Neem Karoli Baba
(Maharaji)

Kol ha Kavod
(All honor and glory)

Delightedly, with sprightly intelligence & play...

I don't know

I love

...A few entries from the log of a human voyage...

Michael Maruti Projansky

Epigraph Books
Rhinebeck, New York

ISBN 978-1-948796-87-3

Library of Congress Control Number available upon request. Contact the publisher for information.

Book design by Colin Rolfe

Calligraphy by Barbara Bash

Epigraph Books
22 East Market Street, Suite 304
Rhinebeck, NY 12572
(845) 876-4861
epigraphps.com

Contents

Dedication

This book is dedicated to Amara, Camala, and Maya, my greatest teachers and teachings. Thank you for taking such good care of me and trying to grow me up.

I won't be here for Asher, Ezra, and Raphael, my grandsons facing all the issues that humans do. This will be a little bit of me in absentia, reminding them to turn cleverness into kindness.

Acknowledgments

Thank you for being my teachers. I can't name all of you specifically but some people have helped me get this book together very quickly. Specifically, Barbara Bash for calligraphy on the front cover; my daughters Amara, Camala, and Maya for the photographs; Zach Rausch for being transcriber and good companion; so to Fred Mayo for transcribing and being a good friend; Bonnie Burgoyne for her incredible typing speed and forbearance; and finally, Jim Ottaway, reporter and editor extraordinaire, and his wife, Mary, who have made this book possible.

Michael Projansky, July 21, 2019

Editor's Note

Michael Projansky has a rare quality of charisma, a fascinating combination of openness and loving kindness to everyone he meets, sharp insights into the mysteries of life and the human condition, and a wonderful sense of humor.

In addition to those lovable qualities, Michael has been tuned to extraordinary wave lengths of perception since he was a child. Like a dog hearing sounds at higher decibels than we humans, Michael has seen the visions and had extra sensory perceptions and insights he describes in this book.

Michael himself wrote some years ago all of the Hospice Visits and Atlantic Voyage chapters of the book.

And he told all the other stories to his friends Zachary Rausch and Fred Mayo who transcribed them faithfully in a short period of time starting in June, 2019. I then read the stories back to Michael for his final editing in his own words.

Jim Ottaway, Jr., July 30, 2019

Preface

"I don't know . . . I love."

The purpose of this collection of stories is to recognize near the end of my life that I have lived an incredibly rich life. Now – thank God – I am so much less self critical, I can appreciate the richness of my life, and I can tell my stories honestly. I am not a man writing spiritual stories; I am a man of spirit writing my life stories. There is a difference.

I have seen teaching from so many traditions. I have wandered the world and found myself back where I started. The whole issue was the distance from my heart to my head and back again – a distance of less than a foot and a half. I have an impulse to go back and say to everyone that I did not love you as much as I could have – I am sorry. After a lifetime of self–doubt and self-criticism, I am tired of that now.

When I was a child, It was very clear to me that I had a job, a purpose, an identity and an activity – all wrapped together. I was on a mission, which was to love everyone. I thought I had failed at that since I did not like some people. Some people were unhappy in spite of my loving. I thought I had failed. I thought I was helping them, but they were still miserable. In fact, I confused my intention with the actual results. Growing older, I lost that clear sense of purpose and got distracted by being a bright, white man. I moved from my heart to my head. And learned the black arts of cleverness.

When I was seven, playing in my school yard, I had a vision of Maharaji, and I knew I belonged somewhere else. I realized I was just a visitor on this planet. Then I saw Maharaji in the sky at 191 degrees magnetic, and I knew that if I could get to him, he could show me how to go home. And I did and that is what has happened in my life and to my life. I met him later in my 20s, but when I had this vision of Maharaji in the sky, I had no idea who he was. When I was in my 50s, I spoke with Maharaji and asked him for a mantra specific to my life. He emphatically stated, "I don't know. I love."

Now, I recognize that without self-doubt and without self-criticism, human life can be an extraordinary celebration. I have tasted some of it and it is extraordinarily freeing. I would love to live my life again knowing what I know now, but that time has passed. It is important to recognize the power of self-doubt. We hurt ourselves by the negative things we say to ourselves. The cure is to be aware of that and not to fight it. Just accept it and affirm yourself.

I remember eons ago, when dear Ananda and I took acid together when we first met, I told her then that, "The greatest crime against ourselves would be to forget what we are learning here when we go back to the gray world." I now know that is not really possible. The game is so much bigger than one human life. Nothing is lost; every insight becomes part of us whether we forgot it or not.

I have been progressively disentangling from being human, and it has been very important to me that you are reading this so that I can tell you how much I love you. I appreciate the help you sent me and all of the love that you have felt for me.

I would have loved all of you much better if I knew how to. For that I both apologize and offer this book. I made the mistake of accepting thought and cleverness for wisdom and in the course of that lost myself to the mind's machinations. There is more than enough cleverness already. What we need more of is loving-kindness. That has been and is the central task of every human life: To change cleverness into loving-kindness for all.

Editor's Note: *Michael Projansky to Fred Mayo, a good friend in the New Paltz morning meditation group, at Woodland Pond on June 30, 2019. Mayo taught Education courses at SUNY New Paltz; was Executive Vice President of the Culinary Institute of America in Poughkeepsie, NY; then Professor of Hotel Management at NYU in New York City.*

Introduction

To my readers: My name is Michael Projansky. I was born in White Plains, NY, on November 22, 1939, which later became co-opted from my birthday to "Kennedy Day" because he got shot on that same day.

Right now I am living in a place called Woodland Pond, a nursing home in New Paltz, NY.

Now I am sitting. I am always sitting. I am limited to an electric wheelchair and a hospital bed. I cannot walk anymore after having lived a very active, and what I feel, a very full life. By my own imagination, I won't make it another six months. So, it is near. I have been dealing with a strange illness for about five years now. There has been a slow inexorable, degradation of my physical capacity, starting with balance, then my arms and now my legs. My doctor calls it a rare form of ALS called MSA (Multiple Systems Atrophy).

But don't worry. I haven't totally lost my marbles. I have lost some short-term memory but I can still think pretty clearly.

What I really believe, really believe is that, right now, I am looking at a picture of Neem Karoli Baba and I feel as though he and Emmanuel, who was Pat Rodegast's (my second wife's) channel spirit, may be the same person because I think of them together, working in cahoots. It's a conspiracy! They seem to be minding my business, or at least I'm imagining that they are, and they have concocted all of this to teach me more and more before I die. As a result, they give me occasional insights which feel to me like entering different realms of existence. They change the way I look at everything. I feel much more benign toward people than I used to feel.

There has been a monk-like quality in me all my life and I now find myself cared for, fed, and without responsibilities outside of myself. It is the perfect place to deepen my practice. This book is part of that. I have come to realize that I have had some extraordinary experiences although some of them seemed ordinary at the time. I am trying to share as many of them as I can with you. This book is dedicated to my daughters and grandsons with whom I would share these stories but I won't be here. I am trying to do it now. My dear friend Zach Rausch is taking this down now. It is great that he is doing this for me.

Editor's Note: *Michael Projansky rented a room in the same house with Zach Rausch on DaVinci Way off Plains Road in New Paltz owned by Glenn Nystrop. Zach got his BA at SUNY New Paltz, with a Buddhist Studies semester in India. He is now a PhD student there in psychology. Zach helped Michael with all sorts of chores as Michael had to move out to Woodland Pond when his illness disabled him in 2017. Zach started writing down some of Michael's stories in May, 2019.*

Original Intentions

When I was a child, I knew that I had been given a particular assignment and with it I had a very clear sense of purpose and identity. I knew what I was doing and it was good. It was a wholeness that I never had since. The assignment was to love everyone without exception. Then I ran into the most destructive force in the universe; self doubt. It said to me, "Can you prove this?" Which I could not. The result was a mild-mannered gentlemanly cynicism.

As I grew up, I became more and more clever, smarter, learning all the tricks of the black art of self-doubt. My competent mind was a handmaiden to this process.

My mind essentially said, "You hang out with me and I will protect you from disappointment. You won't ever be fooled again and no matter what happens, you will be able to say, I knew it all along. I just went along for the ride."

What happened was, without realizing it, I had moved the greatest distance anyone can move and made a pact with the devil, my own mind. The price was self-love. I had moved from my heart, a full foot and a half to my head and suffered the results of it. Fortunately for me, I had kept a little bit of my initial intention intact so that throughout my life I nonetheless tried to love everyone, with all the attendant human mistakes. I had forgotten about the original intention even though I had kept it quietly alive. It was as though I was sneaking around, hiding from myself the fact that I as intended to love everyone.

Fortunately, as I now approach the end of my life, it is as though, my guiding angels are letting me see my original intention clearly again. And where I really reside is no longer in my head but in my heart.

Maharaji – A Childhood Vision

When I was a skinny, little boy of about six or seven, I went to the local elementary school where we had recess as a normal part of the day. I was at recess surrounded by other kids and a few adults when all of a sudden everyone seemed to back away (not from me, but in me). The noise got quiet and I was very much alone. It was clearly an internal experience. A voice came up from deep inside me and it said, "I am not from here." It was very clear that I was here but I was not of this place. I was a visitor. However I had gotten here, I could not go back that way. My mother and father were my mother and father here but I wasn't of them. And that was true of my brothers also. They were my human family. I didn't know where I came from but I knew I was other and I was here indefinitely even though I would have preferred to be at home, wherever it was.

Then I saw in the sky, at approximately 191 degrees magnetic, about half a mile up and a half mile away, an old man over the hill in the sky wrapped in a multi-colored blanket. I knew clearly that if I got to him, he could tell me how to go home; which I wanted to do. It was not God or some visiting angel. We had no particular interaction other than I could see that he was kindly. After a few moments, maybe a minute, things all went back to "normal." And I got on with my day. I may or may not have mentioned it to my mother when I got home that day but I already knew that it was not something my father could easily handle. Somehow, it would become a loyalty issue, which it wasn't. I also knew that the White Plains, New York, fire department was not about to lend a seven-year-old kid all their ladders, and the new helicopters were not going to be made available to me. I was here, so be it.

Because of the business of childhood, I proceeded to forget about the experience over time until many years later when I took LSD for the first time. After a very complicated experience, I found myself in Central Park, in Manhattan, staring at the sun overlooking the Alice and Wonderland Statue from up above a hill slightly south of the statue. I had just begun graduate school and they had been teaching us about perception and the rods and cones of the retina and how they were destroyable and not replaceable. I knew that staring at the sun was one of the ways of destroying the retina but I saw the same old man who I saw as a child some 20 years earlier, this time in the face of the sun. The same voice came up inside me and in a singsong sound it said, "the sun is my father and my father will not hurt me."

My next vision of the old man was in New Mexico some ten years later when I learned that there was a Hindu Saint named Neem Karoli Baba (Maharaji).

1. Ram Dass

Meeting Ram Dass

I was teaching at Southampton College, living in cheap rental housing on an estate in East Quogue when a friend came over and told me I had to listen to a special guy. I tuned into Lex Hixon on WBAI and heard Ram Dass talking about meeting Neem Karoli Baba (Maharaji).

It was clear listening to Ram Dass that he had found something new that I needed to know about – everything we had both tried had not gone anywhere. The stuff we had tried was intellect, drugs, being cool, and the other usual suspects.

Ram Dass' story about Maharaji was different. I did not know Ram Dass at the time but I became a vegetarian that day as a way of signifying a change in myself. Soon after, some months later, I found out that Ram Dass – whom I had known about because of LSD and Timothy Leary at Harvard – was visiting at his father's country farm in New Hampshire. I had obtained his phone number and called him, and we arranged for a visit.

On the agreed upon Sunday, he was giving a talk, and we had a chance to visit later and really talk. With a friend, I drove my van up to the farm the night before. We slept in the back until awakened the next morning by Ram Dass and Krishna Das who knocked on the door and woke us up offering a breakfast of chai and something to eat.

Ram Dass gave an hour talk to 40 or 50 people, and it was pretty clear that he had gone through some of the insights I had. After the talk, he gathered me up and we went to sit on some boulders. We climbed up and sat there to be separate from the group and the busy scene receded. He asked "How can I be of any help to you?" I was conscious of not facing him and sitting at 90 degrees from him. I remember saying to myself, "You have come to be with him; be with him." Very slowly, I turned my head to him and felt like an ancient stone doorway was being moved in my neck. When I turned to face him, his face was open and his eyes were looking at me; we just engaged in meditation with each other's eyes. We did not blink; we were simply opening up to each other – we were practicing a special form of meditation, which I later found out was called Tratak – for ten minutes, which is an eternity. We realized we knew each other in a way in which words would be a distraction.

That is how I met him and how we began our relationship.

He was willing to receive the full brunt of my fear, camouflage, and subterfuge; it was then that I realized I had become too accustomed to subtly deflecting all experience so as not to be completely seen by others.

He was clearly my older brother!

Aside – I remember the summer we spent in the woods at Ram Dass' father's farm just before Amara was born, Ananda and I laughing and Ananda saying to me, "We better get enlightened before the baby comes." And we giggled. Then we came to New Paltz and had baby Amara in January, 1970.

Naropa with Ram Dass

In January 1974, I had two children and a third one very much on its way. There were two male visitors – Ram Dass and Krishna Das – who came to our house in New Paltz. During that visit, as usual we spent most of our time sitting on the floor on cushions. I was sitting on a mattress on the floor with two little girls climbing all over me, making it clear that I belonged to them. Krishna Das laughed at the situation.

Ram Dass said "what are you doing this summer," and I said, "Yes." He said laughing, "I did not even tell you," and I said, "It does not matter, the answer is Yes." Then he told me that he was teaching at a new Buddhist university called Naropa, which Trungpa Rinpoche was opening. Ram Dass was invited to teach, and he needed someone who had most of it together. He figured he would have 100 students, and he needed someone to do the paper work and handle other stuff.

After they had left, he called me back at the beginning of June, when we were supposed to be going out to Boulder. The 100 students turned out to be 1,000, and I had ten helpers.

Amara and I had a wonderful three-day trip driving to Boulder and sleeping in the back of our van. I have an image of driving down the road with her standing up in the front seat beside me. The high point was the two of us somewhere in Kansas having an ice cream cone sitting on the curb in a little town. As it dripped down our faces, we were enjoying this experience of living outside the lines. It was a magic moment, Amara was four or five and I was 36.

The first half of the summer I spent as Ram Dass' administrative assistant with ten remarkable people working with me. At that time, Ram Dass was a leading light of Western spiritual practice, having just come back from his second trip to India.

At another time, I was on a platform with 15 people seated behind Ram Dass. There were 1,000 people in the audience. I noticed a friend of mine also on the platform. We had gotten busted for possessing grass for our own personal use about 15 years ago. We laughed at where life had taken us. He from Riker's Island, the jail, and me from the steps and bowels of graduate school. We went over to each other and hugged. People laughed.

Ram Dass turned around and smiled and kept talking.

At one point during the summer, it was like a tennis match going on between Ram Dass and Trungpa Rinpoche. Ram Dass talking to 1,000 people in a converted bus garage. The next day, Trungpa would speak to the same people in the same place, they did not contradict each other but it was like a ping pong match, both respectful and playful. It was a treasure.

Personally, I thought I had to choose between the two, which was impossible. I did not realize then that my task was to absorb both of them.

When that month was over – when Ram Dass left – I was hired by Trungpa Rinpoche to help design a master program in Buddhist Psychology for Naropa. It was like going from mountaintop to mountaintop. Trungpa had hired us – his people – as consultants, and we knew better. We were actually getting a tutorial by the master himself. He emphasized at the beginning, middle, and end – don't be a nuisance in another person's life. It was the most respectful training I had ever received.

A high point of our time at Naropa was when I was asked to write an article interviewing Gregory Bateson, one of Margaret Mead's husbands, who was there teaching also. We spent a day. He was a master. We danced around our minds in lots of conversation. At the end, I said to him, "the mind is a great deal of fun." And he said, "Yes, but don't take it too seriously." He was a lovely man.

One day, when a meeting broke up, just Rinpoche and I were left in the room together. I turned to him and said with a smile, "I won't tell but I know you are a fraud.' He looked at me seemingly surprised but smiling and laughing. "You are really running a mental hospital under the guise of a university. " We both put our fingers to our lips in the international symbol of keeping a secret.

What magic. I was blessed and I am blessed.

Near the end of the summer, I was invited by Osel Tendzen, Trungpa Rinpoche's dharma heir, to dinner. I was being offered a position equivalent to a colonel or major in his army. I found a way to get around the seduction business. I thanked him and we finished dinner. When I returned to New York, I asked Ram Dass to bless my going to a Buddhist seminary to which I had been accepted, and moving to Boulder. He told me that we had more business. I told him "If you don't bless it, I am not going." He did not bless it and I did not go.

Michael with Ram Dass at Naropa Institute in Boulder, Colorado, 1974

Michael and Ananda after they married in 1968

"Be Here Now"

"Be Here Now" by Ram Dass was originally a book created in 1970 on butcher paper at the Lama Foundation.

Lama had been started just a couple of years earlier by Barbara and Stephen Durkee. Ram Dass was the first spiritual leader at Lama. He had been on a nationwide speaking tour where he handed out free vouchers for the box of items which included some butcher paper.

After some 25,000 had been distributed, it was picked up by a nationwide publisher so we stopped being a factory and went back to being an intentional spiritual community. Through many lives and some fires, it is persistent to this day where it continues to be a center of thought and practice. Many kudos.

We were like a band of monks from medieval times. . .modern and up to date in the 20th Century! I am very proud that there are two of the pages in the original "Be Here Now" book that I hand stamped on butcher paper letter by letter, feeling like an old Tibetan monk having made a painted prayer flag that was being flown on a high mountain pass.

We were a bunch of very bright underachievers and "lone walkers" who found ourselves at Lama where we became strong devoted workers. Various teachers were brought in but its generative force was self created.

A Memory of Krishna Das

Back in 1974, Krishna Das was not very good with his instrument. He is now very good as a world class musician. In 1970 he actually lived in New Paltz — back then he was Jeff Kagel and had a German Shepherd named "eye" or "I" and I never knew or asked which was his name. When complimented on his dog, he said, "I am I's person," a different way of putting it. We traded vehicles for that winter. I had an old van and he gave me his old Volvo sedan to drive, since it was safer.

II. India

Bus Ride

For a devout Hindu, there is a Yatra (spiritual voyage) they must complete which involves essentially places in the north, east, south and west of India. Badrinath, a temple in the north, is built of stones geologists say don't come from there. It is the northern-most part of the Yatra. One takes a bus from a little lower in the mountains to Badrinath up in the snow. I bought my ticket and ended up in the back left corner of the bus which turned out to be the outside corner. As the bus went up the mountain, I saw how dangerous it really was. It wasn't a road. It was two paral-lel tracks on the side of the mountain. The bus had no shock absorbers so that, besides it being very bouncy, it was actually very unsafe.

I kept thinking as we went up, the bus cannot keep doing this. This is very dangerous. And as I looked down the mountain sides, I saw the carcasses of other buses that had gone down the cliff. At one moment, I was looking down the cliffside and the bus started to go over. I could feel in my inner ears that its balance was being broken. In a nanosecond, I had three thoughts. One was, "Far out, here is the way I die; in the Himalaya. Second, "Don't sweat the little shit; you could die at any moment." Third, as I looked down at the green of the cliff side, I saw that it was actually a green fabric made of light. It was not solid. Oh yes, it would catch the bus and our bodies so that we would officially die but in fact, through this fabric of light, I could see Maharaji and Hanuman flying just under the surface ready to catch me as I went through the fabric so that my body would die but I would continue.

Years later, I was relating this story to Emmanuel, a spirit who came through my wife, Pat, and told him this story. She said he smiled and I could hear him say, "Yes, that is true. Don't sweat the little stuff. You can fly at any moment." And at that moment, I had seen that what I had taken as a cautionary tale was actually an opportunity to fly. Many years later, I am about to die and I still believe that I will fly with Maharaji and Hanuman. There, I outed myself.

Bandhara

It was 1976. Maharaji had died three years earlier and I had to go to India to bring my respects. I had a flying phobia; but I forced myself to fly to India with a secret hope that he would manifest himself to me in some way even though he had died. There had been such stories. I was still carrying the weight of not having been with him when the opportunity seemed to present itself some years before. See this one, see that one, go here, go there. So I was pretty much managed as to who, what, where to go in India.

A few days before the Bandhara, which was to be held in Vrindaban down in the plains, I am up in Kainchi, in the mountains under the wing of Siddhi Ma who was Maharaji's leading devotee. We took the train down to the plains and got to the Bandhara, where, still under jet lag, I was given a bucket of vegetables and a ladle and I was instructed to serve people who were sitting and waiting. It was an amazing immersion for me to see thousands of Yogis and to be amusing to most of them, some of whom were outraged that a non-Indian would serve food at a Bandhara (their orthodoxy was offended). But the general belief was that nothing happened unless Maharaji approved. I was astounded to be used as a vehicle of delivering Prasad (holy food) from Maharaji to the people.

Maharaji's Third Bandhara

I went to Maharaji's third bandhara – an annual celebration in September (the month in which the saint died under a full moon) and local devotees are invited and local holy men are invited too. At this event, local yogi are also honored at the event by a deceased saint such as Neem Karolyi Baba.

At this event, I met Ravi Khanna, a young devotee and sweet man, I went to Benares with him and proceeded to get very sick – I lost 20 pounds in ten days and turned yellow. I kept seeing the Indians bathe in Dashashwamedh, a special place for daily immersion purification. They would bathe, take water in their mouth, and spit it out. I watched for five days and thought I did not belong there since I was an outsider and should not usurp – even temporarily – their world and their sacred river, but one day I went in and immersed myself, thinking about my kids, my brothers and their wives and kids and increasingly expanded the circle, in my head, to include the whole world.

I heard a deep voice inside me say, "Ye shall cast your bread upon the waters of your faith." Realizing the Ganges was a dirty river full of effluent, and it is also the river of light that emerges from Shiva's crown in perpetual meditation on Mount Kailash, when I heard this voice, I decided that it was important to immerse myself in the river. I drank a gallon of water and swallowed it. I slowly started getting better over the next few days.

Body in the Yamunah

Along the Parikrama, there were many temples, ashrams, and holy men living along this sacred path. I stayed and hung out with some workmen for an hour or so and then continued after their insisting I take food, water, and hashish with me. After their insistence, about three quarters of the way, the Parikrama continued along the banks of Yamunah River, one of the holy rivers of North India that makes up the Ganges further south. The river was pretty much dried up and the river bed was exposed. A very strong smell hit my nose and was familiar, the smell of death. Soon, I came upon the source of the smell. Down in the river bed itself, just a few feet below me, was a decomposing human body on its side. What was notable about it was that the skin was on the shoulders but going down the body there was more deterioration to the point where it became a bare skeleton. It was on its side in a somewhat fetal position. I climbed down and tried to figure out a way of photographing myself lying in the mud with it. I wanted a picture lying opposite, like a Rorschach design, spooning it and being spooned by it.

Unfortunately, there was no way to remote control the camera to take those pictures and a selfie wouldn't work. This was film before digital. I finally gave up trying and finished the Parikrama path. I told a friend about it the next day and he walked back to the area with me but the body was gone. Very simply and matter of factly, he said, "The body was just for you. Not for me." It was clear to me then that I had wanted to show a seemingly live person a dead body in the same image, showing that I was already the dead body although I seemed to be walking and talking. I had through my life many experiences that were real but I couldn't prove them and I guess I wanted some photographic verification.

Appointment with a Cobra

When I was in India at Maharaji's temple for the third Bandhara, I got very involved spending my time feeding and serving people. It was wonderful. It was overwhelming.

At one point, while I was staying at the Ashram, which was on a thing called the *Parikrama*, the ten-mile circumnavigation around Vrindavan, otherwise known as Krishna's childhood home.

As legend has it, it had been set down or designated by Krishna himself in his boyhood. It is a holy trek which I decided to do.

After the trek, I got it in my head that it was very clear that I had an appointment with a cobra. The snake, when it rears up about three feet off of the ground raises its head and opens its hood. They say in India that you cleanse the sins of a 1,000 lifetimes if you have the full darshan viewing of the cobra's hood; but the cobra might kill you. If he bites you, that is it.

I had an appointment to go see the cobra. And I was going Tuesday at 2 p.m. (which has become an important time for me since then).

As I went to the pre-arranged appointment, I stopped myself and realized that my body didn't belong to me anymore. It belonged to my daughters; they were my children. I realized that no matter what spiritual quest I might be on, I owed them first. It was very clarifying for me to realize that my body was not mine anymore. I had drunk fully of the Gatorade or the Kool-Aid of human existence. I had taken on humanity and I had taken on being a father and householder with pleasure and honor. So I never kept my appointment with the cobra.

Someday after I die or at the point of death there will be a cobra involved, I am sure. How? I do not know.

Love for his three daughters saved Michael from a Cobra in India. From left, Camala, Amara, Maya

Just Hanging Out

When I think of Maharaji now, I have a picture and memories and I also hang out with him. There is a place at his Ashram, at Kainchi in India, where there is a small walk-bridge of cement above a creek. At the end of it, there is a small landing, then three or four steps down to the actual entry to the Ashram. Behind locked gates, I go and hang out with Maharaji on the landing whenever I think to do so. He is sitting on something like a small bench and I am sitting on the ground next to him, on his right. And he pets my head. When I do good, he pets my head. When I do not so good, he digs his fingernails into my head. Painful, not lethal. I am his pet. Sometimes, we are visible, sometimes we are invisible. Every now and then, a job needs to be done. I just simply get up and do it. Helping an old woman or old man. Ordinary stuff. Sometimes, I don't understand it but I am to get really dressed up and go be Maharaji's emissary where I am there to do what Maharaji would do, which was to do very little other than emanate his goodness, breadth and depth. No particular action for me to take. Maharaji and I don't speak but I know that I am in training. Just hanging out is enough. It is permeated with contentment. We are doing what is given for us to do.

Occasionally, when I go to be with him, his bench is empty and I am given the opportunity and responsibility of being Maharaji in those moments when he is not there. This is becoming, almost imperceptibly, more comfortable through time.

Burning Bodies

There is a place by the water called Mani-Karnika where they burn the bodies. Benares is thought of as being Shiva's city. The belief is that if you die in Benares, Shiva whispers the name of "Ram" into your ear as you die. And because you have "Ram" on your mind, you become free of the wheel of incarnation. So obviously, Benares has become a popular place to die.

They have been burning bodies there for 4,000 years. I could not, not go. As I sat among the 30 or so smoldering piles of burning bodies, I was struck with how hot it was. It was all somehow endless. New bodies, ashes thrown in the river, men working. As I sat and meditated, I felt a tap on my shoulder. One of the workmen who tends the fires and burns the bodies was tapping me. I assumed it was to tell me that I wasn't allowed to be there. But instead, he and the other men accepted that I was sitting among the burning bodies and they invited me to eat with them and share a bowl of hashish, which I did with great gratitude. Mani-Karnika is happening at this moment and will continue indefinitely.

Sarnath (Deer Park)

I had gone to Benares with Ravi Kannah (a wonderful young friend and close devotee of Maharaji) where I proceeded to get very sick. We decided to go to Sarnath, which was very close by. Sarnath was known as the Deer Park in antiquity and every Tangka of the Buddha's life shows the deer of the Deer Park. Sarnath was the first place the Buddha had given a public teaching over his doubts that anyone would take those teachings seriously. Now, Sarnath had become something of a theme park; very old, very simple constructions relating to different schools of Buddhism. At one point, while we were there, I became somewhat tired and told Ravi that I was going to go sit by the fence separating Sarnath from the jungle. I sat down and as I glanced through the fence, I saw a group of deer as though they were waiting for the Buddha to return to give more teachings. I felt that I was immersed in legend.

Train Platform

I decided to go to Bodh Gaya, which was in the East on an overnight train ride. It is the place where the Buddha is said to have taken his enlightenment. I went to the train station to buy a ticket. I was informed that it was during monsoon and the train was washed out and there would be no overnight train. It was unclear when the next train would be. In my frustration I thought, "Where am I going to go now at 11 p.m. at night? Find a hotel? No." I went back to the platform and simply laid down with one bag against my head as a pillow and the other bag around my arm to prevent it from being stolen. Then I proceeded to sleep.

In the morning, as I got up, I was fairly proud of myself that my middle-class Jewish upbringing in Westchester County was wearing off a little bit; that I could sleep on a concrete platform. And in an almost celebratory pride, I glanced over to the next pillar on the platform and saw an Indian family getting up and going about their business. I realized that they slept there every night of their lives as a matter of course, and I felt somewhat chastened.

Path to Kedarnath

On a mountain path toward a temple named Kedarnath, I started to develop a fever and it began to snow. I realized that I could not continue but going back was not an option for me. I had once seen a mountain goat in the Himalayas standing on jagged rocks surrounded by ice. I said the goat can go. I will become a goat. So conjuring up whatever capacity I had, I did in fact become a goat.

As I continued on the path, the fever took its toll and I was stumbling by the time I got to a house on the path where travelers could spend the night. I came to the doorway and the man in the place said nothing but took me quickly inside where it was warm. He had me lie down on some quilts on the floor that made a mattress and covered me with more quilts. He then gave me some Chai tea and gruel. The next morning, after about 12 hours of sleep, I was well again.

He made me more tea and porridge and sent me on my way refusing any money, saying that it was his honor to serve pilgrims. I thanked him and continued.

Karmapa

The sixteenth Karmapa was the head of the Kagyupa School of Tibetan Buddhism. He was co-equal to the Dalai Lama who is so well known in the United States. People like that are constantly the center point of events that are fundraisers. They are both committed to protecting and providing for vast numbers of people.

I was a very good friend of a friend of the hosts who gave an afternoon event for His Holiness whom I had a very good feeling about. I was not invited as one of the major donors but I could be counted on for a good question. The protocol of the situation turned out to be the following: There were some 30 or 40 of us on the living room and dining room floor in a very large apartment on Upper Park Avenue in Manhattan. Carpets and cushions had been put on the floor for us but it was also understood that the Karmapa was to be seated in the highest place in the room. The only other chair was a folding chair for his translator. There was a box to receive the donations which were envelopes, food, flowers, or Katas (the white unfinished silk scarves that were handed back and forth at such events). Each person was to give an offering, do a prostration to His Holiness, sit appropriately and ask their question. Under no circumstances were the people supposed to look at the Karmapa's face, but rather keep their eyes down. I had no trouble with this Tibetan custom.

About half way through the afternoon when it was my turn to ask a question, I immediately dismissed the question that I had worked on for two weeks. It was obvious to me to be too cute When I gave my kata and sat down Japanese-style and glanced at his face, it was so beatific and emanating good cheer and open expectation that I couldn't look away. So we sat there, the two of us staring at each other laughing in full delight. It was clear to everyone in the room that he and I were committing a faux-pas. I expected at any moment to be berated for my behavior.

Finally, after a couple of minutes, the translator asked me if I had a question for His Holiness. Not leaving the Karmapa's face, I said in his presence, "All my questions have vanished." Hearing this, he clapped his hands delighted and said back to the translator, "That makes me very happy and tell him that when he dies all of his questions will vanish."

The Buddha gave a great teaching that day.

Orangutans on the Way to Kedarnath

I was feeling comfortable in my stride up the mountain path toward a temple named Kedarnath. When I came around a turn in the path, 50 feet in front of me was a family of a father, mother and two children. They were orangutans. My immediate response was "Whoops." I had ventured into a domain that I didn't belong in. Fortunately, they decided I was not a danger to them so they just crashed down the cliff from tree to tree going somewhere else. The event made me realize what a protected bubble we all live in. Once again, my guardian angel was working overtime.

III. Hospice Visits

Author's Note: *In my visits with the Hospice Doctor Fred Schwartz, I was attempting to explore the space between life and death, to partake of the mystery of dying. It was a sort of last frontier. Now I am exploring that space, that last frontier myself. That willingness to be with people in Hospice care, with them in the face of death, and this now very personal process, have transformed me into a more humble person, more accepting of myself, my friends, and other human beings. I owe much gratitude to Dr. Fred Schwartz for taking me along with him on these visits after which I wrote the following stories. His generosity and warmth was felt by all. I am honored to call him brother. He is a true hidden Bodhisattva.*

Hospice Staff Meeting

There is absolutely too much to deal with in too little time. . .so they press right on, this apparently unremarkable looking group of people doing some absolutely remarkable work.

Stories are told of the couple in their late 80s and 90s who are caught as they try to sneak out of the hospital in the middle of the night to feed their stray cat. . . The Department of Social Services doctor who refused to see one of the hospice people at the hospital. . .The client's complaint about the nurses' aide who "pays too much attention" to what is going on in the apartment. . .The endless details concerning the managing of bodies that can no longer be expected to care for themselves and must be seen to by others.

Within the deliberations there is the full array of the external managing of the subjective experiences of both staff and clients. There being necessarily little time for extended contact and the fact that often only one of the staff has seen the client, much of the discussion involves projecting onto the clients all sorts of motives and purposes that may or may not be those of the client.

What is striking is the general respectfulness with which the clients are treated. The clients are not "guilty" of being ill as they are often seen in other settings. There is not the hidden sense of resentment that many groups of care-givers carry that implicitly says, "If you weren't here in front of me requiring care, I'd be done and could leave and go do something more pleasant."

These people are not going to leave. They are on board the Ship of Compassionate Service and they know the voyage lasts forever. They have all long ago gotten over being surprised or delighted or chagrined at discovering they are crew on such a vessel. There is simply nowhere else to go. . .and they already know that anywhere else becomes the same as this somewhere else. They are where they belong and they know it.

It is not that they don't have their own personal lives. Of course they do, but their work is not separated out in the manner that most feel it necessary to do. The work is not something they have to do so they can afford to go do things they like. Their lives are their work and their work is their life. . .the same thing. Their lives are to care about and to help alleviate suffering.

This all sounds more romantic than it is. . .It's what happens when you don't hide from suffering. . .when you keep your heart open in hell. Hell is still hell, but you know that as hard as it may be, being in hell with your heart closed is really HELL. . .and the nature of us all is that eventually, our hearts open.

So these people go on about their daily work, going into dangerous places, dealing with difficult people, engaging insoluble tasks. After a short while, whatever they think got them here to begin with becomes irrelevant. . .They make connections with the suffering and they are again fully engaged, here, now.

Meeting over, everyone leaves quickly with too much to do. It is now 3:30 p.m. and there are two visits in Manhattan yet to do.

Hospice Home Visits with Fred Schwartz, MD, on 9/25/91

Elaine & Avis

First stop is Elaine in a middle class section of Brooklyn. . .a small neat house filled with the illusion of luxury from discount stores; polyester velvet spreads, gilded statues beginning to peel, too shiny to be real. Pictures taken with comedians and singers from vacations in Florida. Elaine is dying of a brain tumor. Her husband is a salesman for Ford. He is apparently rudderless, awash in his own grief at the loss of his wife and the rending of his life as he has known it.

Elaine is almost comatose and unable to meaningfully answer questions. Fred, the Hospice doctor taking me around with him on house calls, yells questions, but it is clear she is no longer taking calls at this location. She is clearly somewhere else most of the time.

She is unable to use her left arm or leg, there having either been a stroke, or too much pressure on the brain from the tumor. She shows the deterioration of appearance that comes from someone else doing one's grooming. Interesting how quickly the artifice of grooming no longer works when one starts to leave and there is little spirit or interest left to keep up the performance of power. . .sex. . .intellect.

Elaine looks infantile. She has not much dignity left.

There is more a feeling of pathos. . .a not particularly noteworthy person is dying. No sense of greatness stopped in mid-flight.

My fantasy is that she has been a follower. . .unsure. . .frightened. . .looking outward for motivation.

We sit with her without a sense of having much business. Fred does his examination quickly and there is no communication with Elaine apparently possible. (As I type this I realize I could have simply sat with her and listened to whatever might have come from either her or whatever entities are within her, not to fix anything, or particularly do anything, but simply to more fully witness to this dying woman. I didn't and I got that message.)

After a few moments, we go downstairs and speak with Avis, the Jamaican home health care aide. She is sweet, round and 45ish.

She is close to tears as she assures us that Elaine is often much more alert than she is today. . .Elaine is the doctor's patient who has been entrusted to everyone else to take care of. Careful that Fred know that she is doing her job, she is also filled with a great deal of love for this woman we have just seen.

Fred has just been buzzed by the office and goes to call in. I sit with Avis and talk with her about her life before she became Elaine's entire human world. She has a mother who may be dying soon in Jamaica and a son in England she can't get time off to go visit. Her eyes say, "How can I go? Do you see that I am caught in/ by my love? I am loyal. I love her."

She speaks to me. I love this woman and appreciate her love so deeply. . .Of course I would climb into that sick bed to receive the purity of her love. . .her devoted caring. (I met an old man in India 15 years ago who was capable of such love, pure, non-demanding. . .it is nectar that feeds a voiceless hunger, a yearning deep within us for a loving touch from home.)

She looks at me with almost pleading eyes, as though I were the one empowered to release her from this holy bond. She cannot leave until she is released by Elaine's death or some other authority.

I look at her, wishing for her to be free to go to her own son and mother. Let her be free of being mother to these two white children born here of parents from Europe, all so far from her island home.

She shrugs and says, "There is no money. It is better here for money."

Aaah money. What we do to our hearts and each other in the name of money and the structures of human bartering.

Now she is once again answering the call to love, the supreme effort that is no struggle when one is within the flow of the great river, the river of love. What to do when in the recesses of the heart there is the memory of other loves shared before, that are a balm when one is tired and there is no one else there except a partially comatose woman one has just met a few months before. . .a little girl of 45 given over to one's care in the name of who knows what?. . .What to do?

It is an academic question. . .She will stay until released by Elaine's death. Avis is not one given to the sense of personal power and the privileges of choosing to do as she wishes. She has eaten daily of the bread made of requirement and necessity, so she will miss her son and mother and she will sing them to sleep daily in her heart and they will be shielded by her love unaware of her longing. . .Oh Lord. . .what we walk past every day without seeing. . ."I was thirsty and you gave me drink. . ."

Fred is done and has not eaten of this feast she and I have shared. As we go through the door I reach out to her and we hug, both crying softly, thankful for each other and the affirmation we are for each other. We are brother and sister. We are here to honor our heart's loving. It is our blessing and our burden. We smile to each other through our tears. Nothing to be said.

Never again can I see another anonymous black woman in an aides uniform, at the end of a long day, waiting for a bus and not think of Avis.

In the car we search the Brooklyn street map to find the second stop of the morning. It's now 9:30.

Gabriel

Down near the bay, we find the apartment Gabriel shares with his wife, the second floor of a small cottage facing empty lots. As we climb the stairs, his wife yells, "Careful, don't fall." We are careful, we don't fall.

They are seated at the kitchen table. There is a bowl of soapy water, a safety razor and a mirror. As she finishes shaving him, there is wiping, clearing, much talk, impatience, flurrying. . .then it is done.

She helps him walk the five steps to the living room and he sits at the far end of the couch near the window with Dr. Fred opposite him perched forward on the edge of a stuffed chair. Another first visit but it is already obvious that Fred and Gabriel like each other. Fred has the gift of friendly non-intrusive chatter that is also a teaching-healing-reframing-soothing reassurance to anyone who needs the doctor to take over and be kind and Fred is a "nice Jewish boy doctor." Gabriel is the remnants of a tough talking wiry Jewish man. . .big heart hidden in a street tough swagger.

Fred asks questions of Gabriel about bowels, walking, eating, sleeping, and is answered quickly by Gloria. . .with much pride that she can give the right answer. It is clear to Fred that Gloria will keep answering questions.

They want to know why Gabriel isn't having any more treatments like he was having so many of before. Gloria keeps asking, "But why?" as Fred is explaining that the doctors don't think that more treatments will do any good. Gabriel is beginning to realize that he is getting a death sentence from the nice Dr. Fred. He seems ready to hear it, but Gloria does not.

I actively engage Gloria so that the critical communication can be made between Fred and Gabriel. I ask Gloria who the people are in the pictures and she seems pleased to disengage from Fred and Gabriel for now. I listen to hear Fred say, "There isn't anything to do any longer," and Gabriel nods and says, "Okay, I understand."

At this point he turns to Gloria and informs her that there is no point in talking about treatments any longer. The communication between Fred and Gabriel is clearly the point of our visit and Gabriel makes it clear that they are now in a new reality. It is hopeless.

My sense is that Gabriel has known this by himself but did not have enough authority to say so and have it "stick" in the face of Gloria's pleasure/duty of doing, arranging appointments, giving medicine, etc. Fred affirmed it for Gabriel. Now, fully empowered by Fred, he could clearly articulate it for both of them to know it out loud without discussion or argument confusing the issue.

We have been sent as messengers and witnesses to the end of hope for cure in this man and the woman's life. There was a silence after Gabriel spoke and it seemed that they didn't want to talk any more. We stayed a short while longer and then, after Fred's assurances that he would return and that he was committed to helping Gabriel be as comfortable as possible, we left.

Gloria and Gabriel were left to pick up whatever it was that they had left. No longer any illusion of extended future, just a continuation of this here and now, for some unknown amount of time. . .but no more talk of trips to Florida, or anywhere else. . .

Back in the car, it was 10:45 a.m.

Hospice Home Visits with Fred Schwartz, MD
(9/27/91)

Leonard & Mother

We enter the red brick building, a warehouse for brown skinned people, the multi-generational welfare families. The ones that are hidden away in the slums of America. . .the debris of a social machine based too much on greed and fear that leads to closed hearts.

Fred and I had not grown up in or near such buildings. . .Broken doors, dirt, graffiti, men sleeping on the stoops, loud radio music, no grass around the buildings, abandoned car hulks witnessed to where we were. We entered the building with not a little apprehension. These were not hallways we had often walked before and our white skin announced that we were outsiders. . .for most of the people living there, white skin usually brought trouble.

The probabilities of violence were being calculated in our minds without our having to be aware of it. . .the subtle scanning process. . .was this the day when we would be "innocent" visitors caught up in an impersonal explosion of frustration?

The universe's distribution of pain and elation was not something I was privy to. I had not received a telegram from On High that morning with engraved assurance of safe passage. . .

So the murmuring of the mind's low level call to terror was there in the background. . .as a surety to me. We would not be caught unaware. I was already quietly scared.

As we entered the elevator, the strong odor of urine signaled the crossing of a threshold. We were entering a place in which the ground rules weren't clear. Although clearly together, a glance showed we were both immersed in our own private negotiations with fear.

We enter the apartment. The living room is empty save the vinyl covered couch, the TV, a kitchen table and three chairs. There are other rooms off to the left. The sounds of some morning game show fill the space.

These are the notes I wrote later in the car:

". . .Mother – eyes of tears, fears behind sorrows and acceptance. Seeing each thing of love and hope slip away. Knowing that all of it will pass through in a form she dreads. All joy being temporary.

"This child who was frail and early at birth. This retarded child who was not supposed to live. . .has persisted some 21 years. In and out of hospitals and busses and subways. . .no cabs, no money, no relief, no surcease, no ease, no leisure.

"Always concern. . .always sorrow.

"And always too, her love. Behind the sorrow was the love these two have shared. The love born of the promise and the hope of the mother for her firstborn. . .This child who has brought his mother from earth to heaven to hell and back to earth over and over. And through it all there is the abiding, the abiding, the loving presence. . .the willingness to witness the struggle of this flawed child to walk in human form.

"The unspeakable compassion of a loving mother bearing witness to the pain of her child.

"And Leonard, half here, half gone already. . .Exploring newly again the inner landscape he only partially left in order to walk this human labyrinth in confusion. Moving inexorably towards the release from this pain, this cancer which has come unseen, unbidden. Not understood, there is no communication from Mother about this, none being possible.

"There is just the fact of the pain she can only partially alleviate with the medicine given by spoon. Pain grabbing the bowels in a vice so that breath isn't possible. . .again and again the pain. . .'Ma, the medicine, Ma, pain, Ma. . .then finally the body-fuzzing velvet of the morphine.

"Fred asks if she has any questions that he can answer for her. She looks at him for a moment with quiet appreciation for his effort. They both know this a futile struggle with pain. She looks back out the window at the gray day and says, "I already know the answers to my questions. There is nothing else I can do for him."

"A loving wise teacher said, 'Don't you see that it's all perfect?' In this time and place I can't. I don't want Leonard to be a dying prisoner of cancer so that his mother won't also be dying with him. I cannot yet absorb her pain without struggle.

"And as we watch her pour the morphine, Fred and I both see the Pieta, the Holy Mother and the Christ, here in this dirty apartment building in some forgotten project on the outer edges of a Brooklyn most people don't want to know exists. ('. . .I came to you and you knew me not. . . .')

"After more discussion of medication and Fred's assurances that he would return soon and that the Hospice staff was always just a phone call away, we returned to the urine smell of the hallway. . .again with some resistance, only this time, we wanted to stay where we had been, in the presence of an open vulnerable loving heart. No matter the form, one doesn't leave such a presence easily. Stale urine, now part of the scent of love. . .hmmm."

We sit in the car again looking at the street map. Brooklyn, 9:30 a.m. Time for another home visit.

Hospice Home Visits with Fred Schwartz, MD (10/8/91)

Rita

A small apartment on the seventh floor of another project building in Bed-Stuy. The name has become synonymous with danger and fear. As we stand at the bed of this beautiful 51-year-old black woman who has taken to her deathbed with cancer, I think of all the dangerous hallways she has had to walk in this life.

We who have not lived in slums throughout our lives do not know what it means for those who do. What does the world look like for people for whom poverty is a given? Is there any way to know, or do we all just look across to and at each other with nothing but projection or indifference as our guide? I am again asking myself questions I couldn't answer 30 years ago.

Lying on this bed in this tiny room, Rita talks only with the language of one who has solved problems all her life. "I'm working on this" and "we'll stay with it and see" are the phrases that she has used throughout her life. Feelings and emotions are held in check. No softness, no weakness acknowledged, only strength and effort. Fred speaks to her with such tenderness and respect. He knows her predicament better than she. He knows that she is dying and that effort on her part will not beat this cancer which has already consumed her body beyond repair. He knows that the food she eats is taken first by the cancer. . .that the movement towards death is hastened, not toward life. This body is dying. She will not leave this apartment, except in death.

And yet, he listens to her, allowing her words of effort, strength, hope and wellness to move through him as he listens carefully to hear the answers to his questions about pain and bowels and appetite and sleep and comfort, but mainly pain.

As they speak, Rita does not hear from Fred the reassuring words about "getting better" that we all expect to hear from our doctors. Rather, he says things about comfort. Although she hears him and appreciates this man who has come to her and clearly cares for her well-being, he is not central to her concerns which are to get better. His message is premature for this woman of problem solving and no nonsense action. She cannot hear that her life of activity and mobility are behind her.

They speak to each other, but of different realities. There is not yet a meeting of their minds. Oh, this will come about. Perhaps a few weeks, perhaps a month. In the meantime, he will monitor her medication and visit to make sure she's comfortable. And during one of these visits, she will ask or tell him something. . .to signal her recognition of the end of her life coming swiftly. They will then be together in a different way, with an intimacy they don't yet share. . .after the pretense of success has been let go. They will then sit together and witness the business of dying, this black woman and this white doctor.

As we leave, Fred suggests walking down the seven flights and Rita's 19-year-old daughter says, "No, you don't want to go down those stairs. You don't want to know what's happenin' on those stairs. Take the elevator."

Oh Rita where have you been? Where are you going?

Jean

We find Jean in a one-room flat on the first floor of a small ugly house somewhere in Queens. The room looks like 19th Century Italy with formal pictures of posed couples with stiff collars and long dresses on every shelf. Worn carpets and heavy drapes surround 78-year-old Jean who is dying of a brain tumor with metastases all over her.

She sits in a chair like a statue. She might have been sitting like this for the last 20 years in this darkened room. It is like a vision out of a Fellini movie, old, overpowering, immovable. Her eyes have the lidded, soft focused look of one no longer really here. . .one who comes and goes according to some inner monologue rather than interaction with the reality you and I are moving in.

When Fred speaks with her, she is very definite about her responses, too definite. She has begun to lose it and she works very hard at trying to shore up the slipperiness of this reality that she no longer can keep hold of. She says yes to everything in a very convinced way. Reality, this consistent, time limited, logic serving agreement that we are sharing is no longer manageable for her. She alternately retreats behind her lidded eyes or comes forth with an angry complaint about Marie, her home-care aide. Marie smiles and says, "Oh, poor woman, she crazy."

Jean was a child, a daughter, a friend, a lover, a wife, a mother. . .a woman with desires, hopes, pleasures, passions, the full juicy tempestuous tumult of a human life. . .and now she sits in this chair being ignored and attended to by the Polish immigrant woman Marie who comes at 8 a.m. Monday and stays until 5 p.m. on Friday. . .105 hours without leaving this dark apartment. . .with an essentially mute 78-year-old brain damaged woman as her companion.

Marie has no more or less cruelty than any other person, and I wonder, as she hurries to stop Jean from crying, how well I could stay with this woman for week after week? How quickly would I get angry and uncaring?

Jean's daughter works all week and then comes to spend the weekend with her dying mother. On Monday morning she is freed to go to work. Then Friday after work she returns again to this shell of a mother who can no longer be a human companion. . .now only someone to feed and clean and put to bed and get up. . .almost no longer a someone, but a something.

This is not easy to be in. How does Marie do it? The TV goes all the time and Marie eats as she cooks. I look around and see no books or any other obvious diversions. Marie stays in the kitchen as much as possible while we are here. She has the manner of deferring to authority by becoming invisible as a protection. What has she spent her life in terror of?

And Jean sits, painfully lonely in the darkness of this room, of her illness, of her age, of her other children not visiting, of Marie's resentment that she has come to America and must spend her days and nights with this old woman. . .such darkness. She sits and cannot fully be with us who are with her right here and now.

As Fred begins to examine Jean, he opens her house coat to see that there is a tumor distending her abdomen that must weigh 60 pounds. The distortion is so great that she must be in constant pain. Fred asks her if she hurts and she replies as though he had asked about baseball or cereal or the weather. She cannot give voice in a way that tells another what she is feeling, but we can see the pain on her face and the sound of her voice, a plaintive wail and roar of outrage at the same time.

Jean is in solitary confinement. She is in pain and she is alone. It is haunting and terrifying when I begin to try this on. When I feel my way into this and attempt to know this, to tell what Jean lives in, there is no place of comfort. I do not know what this woman lives in, what memories she may have, but there is no mistaking the suffering she experiences from the sound of her voice and the look on her face.

Fred asks Marie questions and it is clear that Marie will say whatever she thinks will satisfy the doctor and bring her no difficulty. . .So there is little that Fred can really learn. . .the daughter must be contacted and more help arranged. And in the middle of it all, Jean sits in pain and sorrow and will die and take with her the secret of who she is now and what she is going through. Are we all so irrevocably and irretrievably alone?

Good morning. It is now 10:30 and time to go visit Lillian.

Lillian

Lillian looks at us with a bewilderment that this is happening to her. It has just been a few months and she has lost, rather than won the Lottery. She is being sent to Death and it is clear that there is nothing she can do to forestall the inevitable. She was good and she is still being punished by this disease of cancer of the brain. It doesn't make any sense to her. She doesn't know the scope of what is happening to her.

Where to begin to try to gain some control? To get some predictability in her situation.

She was an office manager working well beyond her position, making executive decisions from behind the wall of pretense that so many women like her have been required to do. She had been willing to pretend that she only ran the office, knowing that she was in fact the chief executive. She had learned early on how not to frighten the boss with her intelligence. So she asks Fred reasonable questions that focus on body and function. He can give her very little to work with. He knows no more than she the answer to her real question. . .the one that everyone has learned to turn their backs from since it is no longer (if ever it was) given for us to know these things.

WHY?

Why, after working so hard for all these years, after looking after a husband and children, being dutiful for two now deceased parents. . .why now has this come to knock me down on this bed, from which I can go only a few feet to the toilet? Why can I no longer remember? Why does it all just flow together? Moments of clarity that shine briefly, unconnected to anything else. They are seen and celebrated, but then, they disappear with no trace, no way of being sure that they ever happened. No, she does not ask these questions.

Above the bed there is a chart, two feet by three feet with the times, amounts and names of medications to be poured into her. It is like the indecipherable marble plaques on the walls of European cathedrals. "Here lies Lillian who was filled with loyalties to others and quiet yearnings for herself. Her loyalties were not appreciated until after her dying and her yearnings were never fulfilled other than in very brief moments. Her body lies here dead. . .etc."

She and Fred know that she is already on the debit side of the balance sheet. Although she breathes and can say things, she is now too far gone to any longer be among the human busyness that we call living.

Her husband sits at the small table in the living room with a piece of smoked fish on a flat plate in front of him. He picks at it looking for love and nourishment, but there is none to be had. It is over, this life with this woman. She had been wife/mother to him and it had brought him more security than his own mother had. Now she lies on the bed and makes no sense nor move to resume her life. He knows that she is dying, but cannot look at it yet. The questions as to what he will do with himself alone for the first time in his life, are too terrifying for him. (He doesn't realize yet that others will tell him what to do, as they have all his life.)

Fred answers her questions with honesty and great caring for her as she struggles to arrange it all on her desk in manageable piles. But the piles don't sit still and the desk is made of a mist. She will die soon from the tumor that eats up her brain. . .and there is nothing to be done other than to keep her bowels from being impacted and her pain controlled.

Her sister will sit with her and perhaps relive her own memories of their separate childhoods in the same apartment in Brooklyn.

Her daughter, too young to be able to know the substance of a life that is not made any longer of fantasied future, will sit with her seeking out some meaning in it all. She will have questions for her mother, but she cannot yet form them. The formed questions will occur to her during the years after her mother's death. They will come in those quiet moments when the busyness of life is stopped for a moment. She will nod and smile, she will sit quietly crying, she will laugh, she will remember her mother and she will wonder.

Not now, not yet.

Hospice Visits (11/12/91)

Gino

He lies on the bed, curled up, facing away, towards the wall. He is done with this, this human thing, this worrying and wanting. He is dying and there is little time left. He has said what he could say and what could be heard.

Who knows these things? When and why and how you die? Who knows?

The priests, the doctors, the wives? Hah! No, I am lying here dying. I can feel it. They have to half carry me to take a leak. My legs are gone. And I will go too, soon. There is no more strength in me. I don't want to eat. The cancer in my throat. . .it hurts too much. A few weeks and I die. All I want to do is sleep.

Forty-five-year-old daughter Flavia, ah Flavia. She came out of the womb talking and has been talking ever since. She is the voice of immigrant New York, in this case Italian. Her eyes miss nothing and she has judgment about everything and the way you know what she is thinking is that it spills out of her mouth as soon as she can say it. Most of it is tough-guy-sentimental. Some gentle insults bantered back and forth and she feels safe and makes others feel safe.

They have been staying with Gino for the last five days without any help or clear sense of what to do. They have done very well, but are exhausted.

I make a playful comment about lighting a candle to her, Saint Flavia. She laughs and says (referring to her judging tongue) "Yeah, Saint Flavia the Bitch!" We laugh as her mother and daughter both try again to make respectable this daughter-mother who has always been a delight and embarrassment to them all.

She assures them, "It's okay, the doctors don't mind."

The room is filled with bustling noises of love and concern and also heavy sighs and shrugs.

A shrug is not a silent thing. Someone is saying, "I can't pretend any more that I can know or say or do or understand or control anything meaningful about this. This, which always was out of my control, is really out of my control." And as they say it, everyone who hears the shrug (and everyone does) has a choice: "Do I pretend it's just a shrug and we all know that a shrug is silent so there is no need to answer it? Do I see who that is over there and what has just been said by my brother/sister/mother/father? Do I dare to walk into that room? Shrugs can be very loud."

The 16-year-old granddaughter is trying desperately to heal this man with her steadfastness and loving. She is terrified by what is happening and cannot understand why her mother and grandmother aren't as upset as she is. She doesn't know yet how much mourning of another goes on during the relationship and so the end is often not so different from the rest. And in the mourning there is often the relief that this disappointing relationship will no longer have to be maintained.

Three generations of women sit in this room. In the other room the husband, father, grandfather is curled up on his last bed, dying. They seem to love him from such different places. . .the thought comes that they love him in the same way they love themselves. . .with resignation, with tough sentimentality, with fervent wishes, each sitting in that part of themselves and their own lives.

As we are about to leave, I go to the foot of Gino's bed and he is curled up, facing the wall, snoring. I touch his feet lightly and open to whatever might come. Nothing noticeable does. I shrug inwardly at my own unknowing and aloneness.

When we walk outside, I stop and glance at the brick row house facades. . .They look like illustrations in a children's book. . .too small to contain the vastness within them. I realize again that I don't understand any of this.

James

James is 74 and dying of colon, lung and brain cancer. He lies curled up on his bed in his dark second floor apartment. His breathing is labored and his feet are shaking under the blanket. There is a cross at the head of the bed and a prayer to the Mother asking for her compassion on the night table.

Clarence, the home health aide who has been here half days for a month, speaks of him with such tenderness and loving respect. "I be talking to him a lot. . .He don't say much, but he's a good man."

As Fred and Clarence talk, I wonder about this man who spent his life working as a doorman in Manhattan and in a brewery in Brooklyn. So many questions: What mattered to him? Was the Church real to him, or just another extortion racket to which he paid dues? Did he love his wife? His life? Does he resent what has transpired? Is he full and at peace? Did he love his life? Who is he?

He is the shell of a big man. Did he have big appetites? Did he leave them out, or did he fit himself into some container, one that would protect him from both himself and the world? Where did this cancer that is eating him come from? As I stood watching him sleep, I knew that he was not just "a cancer patient." I knew that he was still very much alive, with or without the capacity or inclination for speech.

Mildred

Mildred is an 87-year-old black Cherokee woman dying of pancreatic cancer. She is back in her own bed after two weeks at her adopted daughter Edwina's house. This is where it will be, in her own bed, on her own terms, at her own time.

The hospice doctor had leveled with her that she was dying. No more pretending. No more fighting the good fight to keep Edwina's fears at bay. Yes, it was time to die. Her husband George had gone before her and she was tired of being alone with nothing warmer than what she could conjure up from memory. . .that just wasn't enough any more.

Edwina was pulling at her so hard it could tear her arm out. So frightened and full of the illusion that she could keep Mildred alive out of the force of her own demand. No, death could not be kept away. Her body had been used up.

This once strong tall young woman, so full of power and flesh, had used up all her laughter and energy and juice and delight and passion and anger and tears. There was almost nothing left, maybe 70 pounds, half of what she had been, this handmaiden to the famous white women she had served for so many years. Oh yes it was all gone now, 87 years of it.

So little of it had really mattered except for the passion with George. My, how they had sung together the songs of the body and the heart. They had ridden the magic carpet together, strong and sure in their love, invincible, beyond anyone's power, leaving them all behind to envy the magic the two of them had shared.

There was no way of telling anyone of what they had been together, and to what purpose? She knew where she had been. The world was okay, but it didn't have any longer what they had shared. No, it was time to go home and so she had insisted on returning to her own house, her own room, her own bed. It would be from here that she would leave, and it would be soon.

Back downstairs, Edwina's words came with no pause, no ease, as she desperately tried to gain some leverage over what was happening to her, this dying of Mildred. Oh yes, it was happening to her, Mildred's dying. Mildred had been that magic powerful mother who Edwina had not had as a child. She was so beautiful and full of certainty like no one else. Where else would Edwina experience the safety she had felt with her?

"No, not yet. Please, dear God, not yet. I can try harder. I will give her even more of my energy even though I have almost nothing left. Last night, I curled up with her in the bed and just poured into her as much as I could. If necessary, I'll just sleep in the bed with her every night. I can't let her just die."

As the doctor went to call in to the hospice office, I stood by Edwina and slowly put my arms around her. I just held her as she continued talking. From within her I could feel the tears begin and slowly she became quiet and allowed the tears to come. We swayed together slowly as her tears flowed. I had nothing to say to this 55-year-old girlchild's sorrow and fearful loss. She was allowing Mildred's coming death to be real. She would not be able to hold back the inevitable.

Her love, her futility, her terror at the loss of this beacon in her life. . .what can be said to this? What can be said to the yearning and the longing of this already a grandmother herself girlchild quietly weeping in my arms?

I gently stroked her face, her shoulders, her back. . .oh that I could take from this young child in my arms all the pain and disappointment of her life. . .embodied in the imminent death of her beloved more than mother Mildred. I kissed her tears, I held her gently, this stranger of 40 minutes earlier.

God, what is this about, this opening to each other? What is this unspeakable moving towards each other in open, kind witnessing? Oh Edwina, thank you for bringing me beyond the mind's evaluating and judging. Thank you for calling me, calling me to worship, as though the muezzin had called for all to be witness to Allah, as though the cantor had begun the Shema prayer requiring all to give witness to the Almighty.

Yes, once again the messenger had been sent to remind me to simply allow the heart to love, to bear witness to the unspeakable, the non-understandable, the ineffable truth of loving presence. . .that is who we are.

Edwina sat down, with me at her feet, and began speaking more softly about how much she loved Mildred and that perhaps, as the doctor suggested, she should call her sons to come up from Philadelphia that night if they were to see her before it was too late. She went to the phone and, after getting her son on, asked me to explain what was happening. Oh how quickly the family of the heart gets established! I explained as best I could to this strong serious young man and then gave the phone back to Edwina.

After some final discussion, it became time to go and I went upstairs to have a moment with Mildred. Earlier, I had watched from the foot of her bed as the doctor ministered to her. It was clear that she could no longer see and no apparent communication had been possible.

Curled up on the bed, this eagle turned mortal sparrow was clenched against her pain. A few moments after I got to the bed, she reached her hands out for me. I bring my hands to hers and after a few moments, with surprising strength, she turns herself on her side facing me.

While she is holding one hand, I began to stroke her face very slowly and gently with my right hand. Her beautiful brown skin was almost translucent parchment under my fingers. Her cheeks and temples were hollow, there no longer being any flesh between skin and skull. Her skull was so hard under the skin. I was caressing her corpse.

She looked at me while I stroke her face, her hair, her throat. . .not to bring life force to her, but simply to ease her pain. After a few minutes, she lay back and her body uncurled. Her eyes closed. She was at rest. A few moments later I went back downstairs and we soon left.

She died the next day.

"Thank you to the people whose deaths I have been present for."
– Ram Dass, "Still Here," acknowledgements. Published in 2000.

Agnes of God

Agnes, in her early 80s, is dying of cancer. It is not self-evident since she carries herself with such dignity and apparent strength. But she is clearly dying and she is not pleased with that at all. She speaks of the cancer that is eating her body as if it were a misbehaving child she didn't have much use for anyway. Her sister, mother and father had all died from cancer back in Ireland.

She has the resoluteness of a nun about her. . .that no-nonsense quality all nuns seemed to have had in more traditional times. As I think about this, I look around the tiny efficiency apartment in the project she lives in. There is a small kitchen, bathroom and this living room-bedroom that serves as eating area also. It is so sparse. . .an empty cage for the dying bird. . .a cell for a dying nun.

At the head of the bed there is a Madonna and child, at the foot, a crucifix. She sleeps each night in this, her last bed, between the nurturing Holy Mother and the suffering of a human crucifixion. The room is narrow where her bed is so she is bordered by these two images of a demanding church.

Agnes is remarkably patient with the examination and the discussion of her body. She is willing to live through all of this knowing that it isn't really very important. She'll make do somehow. Hasn't she always made do with the other unsatisfactory experiences of her life? She is a woman, poor, uneducated, an immigrant, not used to fulfillments.

"If you can't do what is required of you in good spirit knowing that the Holy Mother will be proud of you, then shame on you for being so self-centered. . .Don't forget what Christ suffered through for your benefit and look at how ungrateful you are being."

Oh Agnes of God, I wonder what will you see when you are done here. Will you run and play and tell magic stories with your sister that you miss so much? Will you again be a little girl at the kitchen table with your mother, having hot tea on a cold winter's day back in Ireland 75 years ago? I wish it for you.

Please let my wishes for her be real and true.

There is a magical child in this severe old woman who approaches her death with frozen discipline and occasional warm humor. As a child I was terrified by such people. The almost visible personal carrying of the cross was too stark and unyielding for a young boy to do anything but inwardly shrink back.

But now, oh so many years later, having "done a little time" myself carrying the weight of the truth of human suffering, I no longer shrink back and judge out of fear. I see my older sister and bow my head in respect. She has carried what was given with both courage and good cheer. My eyes are beginning to open to the lilies.

Thank you God for most this amazing day! It's 12:30 and time to drive to the Bronx for a staff meeting.

Giorgos

We enter the small spotless house on the edge of the Expressway. Two middle-aged women, the daughters, receive us as nuns to a monastery. The house is sparse, silent.

We speak briefly about Giorgos, the 82-year-old man dying of cancer. The answers are simple, with no attempt to really communicate, only to discharge the responsibility of providing correct information. That done, we are led to the small bedroom where Giorgos lies dying.

The room continues the monastic style. It is empty other than a bed, a chair and a small bureau. At the doorway sits Giorgos' wife. She is dressed in black, another Mediterranean woman in mourning. This image has been enacted for thousands of years. . .the simple home, the man dying and women gathering around to witness and tend to the passing, whether it be birth or death. Perhaps when things get really serious, and therefore very simple and straightforward, the women are present, to do and be what is needed.

The grandmother sits, willing and able for it all to go on around her without apparent participation. She nods in response to questions and answers posed and responded to by others. She says nothing, but is softly present in everything that goes on.

We look at each other for a moment and there is from her a sweet sorrowful smile that says, "Yes, it is now time for this meal. We have eaten so many meals together, this man, my husband, and I. Who could count how many meals, days, how much pain. . .how much respect we have had for each other?"

As Fred examines Giorgos with the help of Poula, the 23-year-old granddaughter, I sit with eyes closed, feeling my way into this room, this reality, this death. I am sitting with this old woman (With some people, it feels a needless intrusion to ask their name. . .they are embodiments of an archetypal form, not to be overly personalized. Such felt to be the case here. . .no artifice, no embellishment.) Like a rock in the desert. She simply is and this death is. . .no pondering and speculating. . .simply this, now.

She and Giorgos have watched many die during their lives together. There has been much suffering in Greece during the time of their lives. Hunger, war, sickness, childbirth, much death to witness. . .and now it is his turn to die and hers to bury a husband. She sits and watches daughters and granddaughter tend to this man. . .knowing some of his secrets which will die with her. . .and knowing also he had secrets he kept from her and now will never be shared. He is still hard, this man who is like the small island rock they came from.

She sits, knowing that when the doctors have gone, when the daughters go and attend to the rest of their lives and Poula must again take up her life, she will sit closer to his bed. She will sit in silence. She will be there for whatever he needs or brings himself to ask for. . .as she has done since they married back in Greece. . .as children, knowing nothing, some 65 years ago. She thinks: "Parents dead. . .brothers, cousins, sisters all dead. So many back there along this road of work and delight and tears and pain. . .all gone. . .a blessing and a curse. . let this man die with no more pain.

There has been a full share, yes, a full share. And when he is gone, it will be soon enough my time for death. I will be here in this house, or I will go to the other daughters' houses to wait for death. Let it come soon. It is time. I am finished here with whatever I was to do. Now I am only in the way, a burden."

I sit, as invisibly as I can, with this woman as she teaches me silently, nodding.

At the bedside, Poula translates seamlessly back and forth from English to Greek and back again. As she does, she moves back and forth between "the old country" and her life here in Queens. . .school, hope, excitement, life, duties, sex, money, possibilities.

There has been so much death for her. . .three relatives during the last year. It has seemed that life is an endless caring for and burying of one after another.

"Is there nothing but dying? When will I be able to live something other than the honorable duty of tending to the dying? And I have loved this man so much, this form who is no longer my grandfather, but an old man dying. I hate that there is nothing I can do for him. . .I cannot will him 50 more years of life so he won't die before me as he is doing now. . .and sitting there is Grandma who is waiting to take his place. Will I be here in this room a year from now with this same doctor translating for her? Ohh Ohh Ohh!"

We are in a small simple house in Astoria, Queens, a primarily Greek enclave carved out of the mixing of America. . .but more than that we are on the small island back home and everyone on the island knows that Giorgos is dying. Those who have loved him sigh and remember with fondness both his life and the lives of all who they have loved who have also gone. . .the others murmur the appropriate words to show respect.

After the examination, the daughters thank us and lead us to the kitchen. There are questions Poula needs to ask for the family. . .questions about the giving of medicine (at this point primarily morphine), how fast the deterioration is expected to be and whether a son who is tending someone else dying in Greece should come home now.

Though being here for many years, the daughters speak little English, so Poula translates. She sits in the center, translating between languages, generations and cultures. She is the first born of this land. She is the only one who really lives here. . .the others still live in Greece. The bodies may function here, but they have not been distracted by the carnival of America.

We speak kindly and lovingly to this delightful and loving granddaughter, our respect and appreciation of her clear for all to see and know. She is a bridge for us all and it is an honored place in which she sits. We all thank each other for the meal we have shared. . .this gathering and witnessing we are doing. I move to the grandmother and lightly touch her shoulder. . .smiling, she silently nods. We leave.

In the car, we nod to the fact of having just been in Greece for an hour. Neither of us wants particularly to return to New York, we are glad we're with each other. We aim the car towards Manhattan.

Hospice Home Visits in Brooklyn and Queens with Bonnie Weissberg, MSN (10/3/1991)

Jessica, Jonathan, Jason

Bonnie and I take a gypsy cab to a 15-story project a few miles from the Fort Greene hospital. We are in another section of Brooklyn but the energy is the same. Poverty is solidified here. Escapes, if any, are usually to another part of the Nation of Less.

We are visiting a family of five children (5 through 12) who are living with their grandmother, grandfather, aunt and uncle. All of the children are HIV positive and three have begun to show AIDS symptoms. Both the mother and father have already died from AIDS (IV drug use being the likely cause).

It is not clear but the belief is that all five of the children have received the HIV virus sexually from the deceased father. . .(and what do you do with that one?)

Bonnie has come to check up on medications, clinic appointments and the like. When we enter, it is clear that Bonnie is deeply appreciated and the children immediately begin to show her things and be proud of this and that. She receives and touches it all with obvious pleasure and loving respect for them. The energy in the kitchen where we sit is too full. Two of the younger boys (the two with AIDS) begin to climb all over me and I once more delight in simply being a moving jungle gym. I look at the boys and marvel at their relentless movement. They are competing and showing off for Bonnie and me. Will they die before this river of energy slows to a more reasonable pace? What will happen to these two creatures climbing me as though I were a tree?

The older daughter Jennifer (12) has been pointing out the window to family members announcing that she sees her father walking by and why doesn't he come up to the apartment? Along with this she has been crying a lot and hitting at her abdomen. Everyone is very concerned about this, and what does Bonnie think? As this is being discussed, Jennifer is crying again and I am delighted that I don't have to say anything that sounds erudite. It is clear to the adults what is happening to Jennifer and Bonnie's loving comments both to and about her reassure her that she is a good person and she is not to see herself as having anything "wrong" about her.

Through her helpfulness, Bonnie has clearly become very important to this torn family and I am grateful to see it all. The psychologist in me is struck by how unanswerable "professional" questions are. There is nothing to do with any of them but to open your heart and speak simply, which Bonnies does.

Since Bonnie has asked the cab driver to return at 4:30, we need to leave so we don't miss him. Bonnie has cleared up the misunderstandings about medication, clinic appointments, and has attended to the family's concerns about Jennifer. There is nothing else to be done that would take any less than all of Bonnie's and my efforts for the rest of this incarnation. Since the cab is due in five minutes, we leave, after many hugs and picking-ups. The children physically pull at us and attempt to block our exit. The same smell permeates this elevator as in Leonard's building

Back on the street, the cab is not there. We discuss how long a walk it is back to the hospital and agree that we don't especially want to have to walk, but there are no busses here. Well, we will wait another ten minutes and then begin to walk.

I look back up at the building and wonder about how many HIV positive children with dead parents there are in NYC and how invisible they are until they begin to show AIDS symptoms. . .and how many 12-year-old girls have visions/hallucinations of their fathers down on the street? And how many men watch their grandchildren die from AIDS, communicated by their sons through means they practiced on that son when he was young? And how many grandmothers live with these grandfathers and grandchildren knowing about it all? How many? How many family stories that would tear apart the "Father Knows Best" illusions that have been pumped into us?

How deeply can you let this in? Without jumping into rage or knowledge as a deflection? Can you really eat this meal without tearing your heart apart or going bonkers? What do we do with the pain? What do people who live these lives do with the pain? I suppose I'll find out some of it.

Just as we get ready to walk, the cab comes and we both feel a substantial relief. Did he return because we had tipped him well on the first trip? Because he had no other fare? Because he had concern or us? Who knows? I glance up and see that his license shows a French name. A black man with a French name. . .probably from Haiti. Yes, I can hear the accent. And what has he seen. . .here and in Haiti?

There is no point in returning to the hospital (5 o'clock) and so we go to the promenade in Brooklyn Heights. It is near my subway back to Manhattan and fairly close to where Bonnie lives. We sit silently for a while.

We begin to talk about the five hours we have been together and I cannot begin to communicate to her my respect for what she does. There is a simplicity to her compassion that feels very "New York" to me. It's that "I don't want to talk about why I do this almost unbelievable thing that I do. I just do it. How can I not?" Although as we talk, it is clear that we have some different things to chew on for ourselves.

She walks me to the subway and within five seconds of parting, we are both faced with getting safely home. Oh New York, Oh Life, Oh God.

Ellis

Ellis has lived more than 25 years in this same apartment on the Upper West Side facing the river. He and his wife had their children here. . .had dinners for other faculty, students, friends. They have left here and returned here through so much.

In early July, two months ago, he left for surgery. . .and returned home a week later. . .to die. He has returned to the same living room where he told jokes, had animated discussions, watched the 1951 Army-McCarthy hearings, football games and Kennedy's funeral. Now he watches his body shrink, consumed by a voracious disease he cannot cure. He is confined to a hospital bed in the living room, surrounded by the artifacts of a very successful academic life. It's all for naught. No solace is drawn from any of it. It is a collection of empty shells, just as he sees himself.

He and his wife have gathered some literature on new chemical and surgical research being done on the type of cancer he has, but he knows he's going to die. For him the only real questions are: How soon will I not be able to walk?. . .this ex-squash player. . .When will the toxicity in my blood stream begin to scramble my thinking?. . .this professor emeritus. . .Will the persistent pain get to the point where I'll be reduced to a whimpering little boy?. . .this knowledgeable man who reveled in his powers. . .Will I ever again be able to eat a meal?. . .this man of prodigious appetites. . .Will I be reduced to bedpans?. . .You know, real questions.

I look at him and feel his goodness. Oh yes, he has lied at times, the occasional petty cruelty, the momentary closing of his heart. . .the usual human dancing and stumbling. He has lived a life primarily in the cathedrals of the mind. . .classrooms, journals, conferences. . .and has done it successfully, not without considerable self discipline.

As a child he needed to bring some order out of the terrifying and unmanageable world. To create an island of refuge wherein he could feel some measure of predictability, of safety. . .and he did. He was protected somewhat by success, structure and a submissive wife.

And now it's all gone. The whole structure is now suddenly gone. The body hardly works. His mind focuses only long enough to realize that he can no longer truly focus. His wife is there hovering, busy with effort. Her own pain and unanswerable need for reassurance. . .an obligation he no longer wishes to carry.

He has done his best, this man. Are there moments he would like to have back? Of course. As we get up to leave, I say to him, "You are a good man. I'm glad I got to meet you."

He responds saying, "How can you know that? You've just met me."

Merciless mind, demanding assurance and proof of the heart's simple knowing. "I have been with you long enough to know inside," I reply.

At the door Fred asks if his wife has any questions and she pulls back into a cool formality. No there is nothing she wants to know.

Fred has brought bad news and she wants no more familiarity with this bringer of bad tidings.

Back in the car by 5:30 and we have one more visit midtown.

Brooklyn Hospital Hospice Visits with Bonnie Weissberg, MSW

Steven

I hang with four-year-old Steven who begins to play with me very easily. He takes me in without any fear or hesitation. I am a pleasant jungle gym on which he can play. He comes to me and leaves me to go off exploring other kids in this bare environment.

When he is elsewhere, I notice the TV noise. There is some daytime pablum on that is alternately a quiz show or a soap opera. The juxtaposition of the reality everyone is dealing with and the idiocy on the tube is dizzying. I realize that it is a pleasant diversion for the patients. . .but the unreality of it makes me just shake my head and wonder. Steven is now standing on my thighs, exploring my face. Little fingers in my hair, eyes, ears, mouth. I guess I'm okay since he half eats me, laughing, half spitting, pulling at my mustache, nose and hair. I feel glad that I have been found worthy by this little boy who will probably die within a few years.

I hear my mind in the background wondering about this little boy, so full of life and yet so sick. There are no clear questions. I am reduced to another open wondering. I feel so sad at one moment and then full of joy at another. My feelings come and go and he comes and goes. They follow whatever rhythm they do. No, I don't think that he knows my mood and comes to me to change it. We play. He comes, he goes. I cry inside, I laugh. It all just goes on. I love that there is nothing I have to perform here. Just playing with this delightful and beautiful little boy.

Arrangements are made for the doctor to see Steven later and Bonnie spends some time with Steven's 17-year-old sister, Kisha. According to the grandmother, Kisha, who has been sitting nearby showing no interest in Steven, has been very worried about her mother and wants to get back home to Pittsburgh to be with her. She says that her mother does better when she's home to look after her. . .the mother shoots up less heroin and does less prostitution to pay for it. . .all this at 17.

Nicole

We come to a small open ward where there are perhaps ten beds along three walls with the nurse's station on the fourth. Bonnie discovers that one of her clients is indeed there. Nicole who is dying of AIDS. She is in a pediatric hospital bed and is relatively large for the bed. It looks like she is locked in a cage. Her wrists are strapped to flat paddles the length of her lower arms so that the IV tubes will not be displaced and she can't pull them out.

While Bonnie goes over to talk to the nurses and doctors, I stand by the bed and look at Nicole. She is turned away from the room and is looking off blankly at whatever is real for her. Her eyes have a look of absolute hopelessness in them. . .the look in the photographs of mothers holding dead children we see in magazines right after a calamity. . .or some insane bombing run that creates "collateral damage." I have never seen these eyes before in one so young. Nicole is perhaps four and she looks very old. . .and very sad. I stand at the foot of her bed quietly.

After a few moments I feel the need to somehow bless this child and move my hand onto the bed and very lightly touch her foot. There is no movement from Nicole and we are there. . .she apparently oblivious to me and me doing what there is in me to do. . .stand in silent what? Sorrow, pain, commiseration, blessing, partaking?. . .I don't know. I am unable not to touch her in some way with my loving.

We are there in the silence for perhaps a minute or so when Nicole turns her head towards me. Her eyes are clearly focused on me and she begins to move her body up towards me. I cannot reach into the bed beyond holding her hand. I am stopped from going any further by the mechanics of the bed, the tubes and the fact that I am a stranger in a part of the hospital I don't belong in. We are frozen there in this pose. . .she reaching forward, yearning to be taken up in my arms and flown away to some warm beach filled with sunlight instead of the neon grey in which she is imprisoned. . .flown away to where she is young and gay and full of play and joy. . .where she is not mourning, sitting Shiva for her own life at the age of four. . .and I stand there, inadequate to the task that demands magic of me.

I can only be there in my loving and it is clearly not enough to fulfil her desire. Her mouth opens and I wait to hear what will come. She begins to scream and scream. . .but no sound comes out. She continues to look straight at me as she screams and screams. . .not of pain, not some short-term irritation. . .she is wailing. This continues for perhaps a minute. . . so easy to write. . . words on a page, they reflect a complete contraction of her body and a thrusting out of so much pain. The withering of life into death at the beginning of her ascent to life.

This child before me in the bedcage is screaming and wailing and there is no sound. . .She has cried and screamed so much before that she has no more voice. There is no more expression left for her pain and despair. She has no more voice left to declare the outrage. Her eyes demand that I do more than simply stand mute witnessing her imprisonment.

I feel inept as I stand before her. This world is a mystery to me also. I am a stranger here. This has never made sense to me, this world. At one time I believed that knowledge would some day banish suffering, but I came to see that suffering would continue regardless of knowledge, and I became a dropout from the army of knowledge. . .so I cannot see that I am much good to this dying child. . .I can be willing to walk into the space in which she suffers, but can be sure of no benefit that I bring.

I am seeing how the notion of coming to understanding, or resolution about things like this are patches we put on to cover the gaping hole, the great empty space that presents itself when a dying child screams what is too great to be understood.

I realize that until this moment rational understanding had always been the gold medal. My belief was that right and skillful action would come after understanding, and one had a responsibility to right action. Understanding was too often the prize – understanding the thing rather than being more deeply with and experiencing whatever it was.

Understanding is less intimate, less direct, less immediate, less personal. One can understand without having to go beyond the safety of not being fully present. There is another level of relationship to events deeper than understanding. There is a wisdom in which there is no longer the separation that understanding implies. There is no subject and separate object. The subject and the object are one. . . I had never thought that understanding was a consolation prize given for the pain of separation. I used to think it was *the* prize.

Nicole turns away and returns to wherever she had been before we came. I am left just looking at her and wondering. My mind jumps around trying to make some sense of what I have just seen. It can't. A few moments later Bonnie returns and we leave.

Margaret

Margaret is 83 and has pervasive bone cancer. She was "supposed" to die two years ago and she delights in having confounded the doctors for so long. Fred is more a co-conspirator than her doctor.

Her apartment is one room approximately 10 x 18 with small kitchen and bathroom alcoves. There is nothing in the room beside the big hospital bed, a TV, a small bureau and a night table covered with all manner of health food supplements and various vitamin pills. Margaret very gaily tells us that these and God keep her alive.

Her reasoning is simple and quite clear: The supplements are good for her because look at the good she feels. And God is clearly keeping her alive or she would be dead. She is quite emphatic about this latter point. If God wanted her dead, she'd be dead. . .and since she's alive, God wants her alive.

She makes a point of checking to see if I agree with her reasoning about God's keeping her alive. I emphatically do and tell her so. I suggest also that I think Fred's helping God out and she agrees.

This is perhaps Fred's fifth or sixth visit and it is clear that they love each other. He reminds her that they are betrothed and that she needs to get better. He enjoys with her that she "has proved the doctors wrong." There is play and then a quick exam and he agrees with her that she needs a health care aide a few more hours each day and he will arrange for that to happen. After a few more minutes, we are done.

As we leave she specifically asks us not to close the front door so that people can visit her. She makes it clear that she has no fear that anyone will hurt her or steal from her ("I have nothing anyway").

Her play and delight with it all is so contagious that Fred and I feel almost no fatigue. She is a delightfully looney old lady who happens also to be very wise and full of clear faith. We have again been taught that if one is present without expectations or judgments, there is beauty and wisdom everywhere.

Thank you, God, for most this amazing day.

Joselito

At a different time, I was working at Sloan Kettering as a volunteer in the out-patient children's section where kids would come and get their IV injections all day long. From the outside, Sloan Kettering was imposing and the symbol of modern medicine. Inside was something else again. Oh so very human.

When I met him, Jose Bolanos, was a 12-year-old boy being treated for some cancer. He adopted me and I became his big goofy fool. It amazed him how bad I was at playing a new game called Pac-Man. He occasionally would hit me and I would laugh. We were real buddies and he would grab me as soon as he saw me and hold my arm to make sure that I would not walk away. We played pool and ping-pong together, among other games.

One day when I went there, I was told that he was in-patient and had taken a turn for the worse. I quickly went to his room where he was in bed and his mother, father, and parents' relatives were jammed in a small room. I didn't want to intrude but they waved me in. The mother had seen us play together. I sat at the foot of the bed and very lightly took his feet in my hands to bless him.

His father, a pilot at home in Peru, who had brought his family to New York and was driving a cab was saying to him over and over: "Joselito! Joselito! Joselito!" in a pleading manner. He was heartbroken. I closed my eyes and saw Jose after death, having become an eagle up in the mountains of Peru, greeting his father there by simply being part of that extraordinary nature. I said to the father, "He will meet you in Peru." I had also seen that they had a cabin up in the mountains where the father, bereft, would go. I was honored. Honored by being there and getting that vision.

Author's Note: *My loving thanks to all the people described here.*

"i thank You God for most this amazing day"
by e.e. cummings

i thank You God for most this amazing
day: for the leaping greenly spirits of trees
and a blue true dream of sky; and for everything
which is natural which is infinite which is yes
(i who have died am alive again today,
and this is the sun's birthday; this is the birth
day of life and of love and wings: and of the gay
great happening illimitably earth)
how should tasting touching hearing seeing
breathing any—lifted from the no
of all nothing—human merely being
doubt unimaginable You?
(now the ears of my ears awake and
now the eyes of my eyes are opened)

e.e.cummings
1894-1962

IV. Atlantic Voyage (Circa 1990)

Sunrise

It's 4 a.m. and I'm sitting in the cockpit of a 50-foot sailboat about 1,000 miles southwest of the coast of Africa. We have been out about a week or so, and have had the usual: crew getting used to living with each other, working out the food preferences, requirements, seeing how well we can sail this steel beast which is just out of the yard. This is essentially its maiden voyage and we are sailing from Gran Canaria to St. Lucia in the Caribbean. We have another 1,700 miles to go.

I wonder how I got here. A few months ago I had heard that Gran Canaria was the staging area for sailboats that had spent the summer in the Mediterranean and wanted to be in the Caribbean Islands before Christmas. So, I had bought a one-way flight and had been walking the docks for a few days asking everyone for a ride. I finally got a ride and moved on board. The custom was that you came on board, shared the food costs and were expected to be competent crew.

Although well into middle age, I was very inexperienced. I had sailed only for about three or four years and had done day sailing only on smaller boats within sight of land, never having slept on a moving boat, let alone off shore.

Interesting, watching my body getting used to the constant movement, containing a light sense of nausea until one day I threw up over the side and felt completely clear, similar to the fourth or fifth day of a fast, when many of the toxins had been discharged. At those moments, it feels so good, that one is tempted to never eat again, just to keep the empty unencumbered feeling going. There is a brilliance to everything, an immediacy, and with it a sense of gratitude for being alive and witnessing it all.

I had come aboard assuming that the owners and crew were skilled enough, having chosen to set sail across the ocean on a new boat. I certainly didn't feel competent to organize such a venture, and since they had, I assumed their competence. Oh boy! It was clear pretty quickly that they were a mess and I had made a very big mistake. No structure, no procedures, no sense of safety concerns. Just keep plowing ahead.

I figured that they were more experienced and skilled and I would just learn a lot and fill in as well as I could. A few days in, I knew that only one of them really knew anything and he thought he was running the boat alone. It was stunningly crazy. Most things are just mediocre or even tiresome in their craziness, but this was stunning. After all, your life is at stake. We would go from one emergency to the next, without any impulse to work out procedures or responsibilities. The only thing worked out was the watch schedule when each of us would have a three-hour stretch alone at the helm. If help was needed, it was understood that the next man on watch was on call.

Oh yes, did I mention they were alcoholics? I asked about drinking before we left and they said it would be a dry boat. Then, the night before we left, a delivery truck brought 25 cases of beer, two cases of wine, and six bottles of brandy. This for what was expected to be a 21-day trip. I should have gotten off then, but I was broke, had already kicked in my $250 share of the food, and was basically greedy for the ride, not having found an alternative. I had lived through a lot of foolishness in my life so I figured I'd get through this somehow. I guess I was a little bit stunned by my own craziness. Hmmmm.

None of them could cook since they had all gone from mother to wife to divorce to waitresses at restaurants. Astounding how helpless they were when it came to food. They could make a sandwich or pour cereal into a bowl, but beyond that, they'd starve. Putting heat to food mystified them. Having been a single father raising three daughters, I had learned how to feed people so I became the de facto cook on board.

When you set out across the ocean on a boat, there's no room service, so you have to be mindful of how much you eat, and be careful to monitor your food stocks. There just isn't any more out there, unless you get real lucky fishing, and we had no such gear on board.

One day I came back aft from being forward at the bow to discover sandwiches had been made and the youngest guy and the biggest guy were having an eating contest! Stunning in their stupidity. The bigger one laughingly complained for the rest of the day that he had a stomach ache. I came to see that they were BIG BOYS.

What fool had gotten me into this?

No one wanted to do the late watch so I took it with pleasure. . .it was quiet and it was a chance to be awake and not have to deal with any of them. The deal was that whoever was on the helm could decide what music was played, and bad rock and roll doesn't get better when louder. So the late watch had multiple benefits, primarily the quiet.

As I sit, I do a 360-degree scan of the horizon to see if there is any traffic. Nothing. Out here we are very much alone and we probably won't see anything until we start to approach the shipping lanes that run up and down the eastern coasts of North and South America. We will also start to see the looms of light emanating from the inhabited islands of the Caribbean chain, but that is still ten to 12 days ahead. For now, there is blackness all around. It feels absolute. The sky black, the sea black, the horizon black although I can't really see the line separating ocean and sky. Strange feeling to be simply floating as through in space.

Michael doing 360 scan sights a freighter a mile to port

In this darkness, there is the noise and movement of the boat and a sense of speed through the water, similar to being on a jet plane at night. It can also feel as though the boat is simply being buffeted and that no real movement is being made. We depend on visual changes to measure our progress.

I remember driving on the Arizona desert. I was on top of a large mesa and looked perhaps 30 to 40 miles ahead to see another mesa and the black strip of roadway snaking along the desert floor towards it. I drove down onto the desert floor and there was almost no sense of movement since nothing seemed to change. There was noise and slight buffeting of the car, but no sense of progress. Then I could feel the road begin to rise and I realized we had actually begun to climb the next mesa. This sailing was similar and even gave more of a sense of suspension and isolation. A quick glance at the knot meter shows that we are in fact moving, albeit at about six miles an hour, the usual speed for a sailboat.

A strange business this. We pack ourselves into these little tubes and push off from what is familiar and seems safe and float off into water space. Most of the time the movement is imperceptible and then eventually we hopefully find ourselves somewhat near where we are attempting to go.

There is no light except for the very dim glow of instruments that have been dimmed so as not to hamper night vision. All of a sudden the depth sounder begins to flash that we are in ten to 15 feet of water. My breath catches and my heart begins to pound. We are about to crash into something and there is really no safety net out here if we hole the boat and it goes down. Most of the marketing hype for safety gear is aimed at fostering the illusion that coming out here isn't a preposterously foolish and dangerous thing to do.

My mind races to scan every map I have seen since I was in first grade to remember if there are islands out here, knowing that there aren't, trying to remember reading about voyagers coming across uncharted reefs, sand spits, anything. My body starts to move quickly with no destination, but impelled to move fast and decisively since we are clearly in danger. Within 30 seconds it dawns on me that we have probably gone over a school of fish and I glance again at the depth sounder which is placidly again showing the flat bars that signal that we are off soundings, in deeper water than the instrument can distinguish. In this area probably about 2,000 feet of water. We draw approximately eight feet.

I breathe slowly and deeply trying to calm my mind and body and settle back into the cocoon of quiet darkness and gentle rocking. This cocoon is both a haven and a danger. If I get too comfortable, I could fall asleep and that cannot be allowed. On a crewed boat, falling asleep on watch is the closest thing to a capital offense. You just don't do it. There are others sleeping below who are literally entrusting you with their lives. Legend has it that falling asleep on watch was sometimes dealt with by throwing the offender overboard. On later voyages, I learned to move around, do checklists, go below to do something, anything to keep myself awake.

I feel such a welcoming of the change since it signals that I have in fact, kept the vigil through the night. There is gladness and a soft pride. I am glad in myself knowing that I am dependable. I will do my job, I will fulfill my promise. I have kept the covenant. This has been important to me throughout my life. I have measured and graded myself often on how well I have done whatever I said I would do. Shame coming swiftly and sharply to me when I could/would/had to admit that I let someone down, that I had reneged on a promise. The youngest brother having to prove that he belonged, could be counted on, could be trusted for more than fetching toys/tools? No wonder the ocean is cluttered with debris. Look at all the stuff we're each carrying.

Night is not over, but day is in fact coming. During the long night, there can be a questioning whether the age-old ritual of night then day might be different this time since the usual instruments of continuity seem to apply less out here. I have kept my covenant with my shipmates and the universe is keeping its with me. Seems like a pretty good deal. That had always been my deal with the universe. I would do my job as well as I could. I would be as honest and kind and dependable as I could be and the world would treat me decently. With few exceptions, it has seemed to work out that way.

I lock the wheel to keep the boat roughly on course while I go down below and heat up some stale coffee and return to the cockpit seeing that in just three minutes the eastern horizon is getting even lighter. I feel in a rush to straighten everything up because the great human daily enterprise will start soon with the coming of the dawn, and I have held the world in my hands through the night and it is time to hand it off to my shipmates to carry its continuity through the next period of a second, a day, a month.

I feel such gratitude for all those who simply do what is necessary for the benefit of others, the nurses and aides of a thousand types all over the globe. Pettiness and resentment are not part of this. Every one receives with gratitude and there is no carryover of accounting from the previous day. It is all fresh and clear. My goodness, this stale boat coffee tastes good in this moment. I even feel some affection for the drunken louts who sleep below.

There is a Cummings poem that starts with . . ."I thank you, God, for most this amazing day. . ."

A Sailing Sisterhood

I have done a number of things in my life; never really a master in any of them; but I was adequate. I am a master of adequacy; more of marginal competence.

At one point I found myself on a sailboat crossing the ocean with four others. We all took shifts on the helm during the journey. During my shift, which nobody wanted because it was in the middle of the night, I was always left alone. It was amazing. I remember being alone in the cockpit, four o'clock in the morning, doing my 360. There is a habit out on the water that you have to do 360-degree scans to see if anyone is gaining on you or you on them. As I was doing 360s, in the East I saw the black of night covering the horizon. The ocean and the sky were just deep black. Nothing more. A few minutes later, I did another 360 and it was a little bit lighter. I did it again and then it was a bit lighter and lighter and lighter. I kept being aware of this until it was clear that the sun was going to come up in the East. Fancy that.

I became someone who was carrying all of humanity on the vessel. Everybody was under my vision. I was keeping the vigil for everyone. I was the guardian and caretaker. I was completing the covenant between God and the whole universe and myself. If I kept the covenant and didn't crash the boat, the sun would come up and it would all continue.

As it got lighter and lighter and lighter, I saw all the women around the world. I saw an incredible panoply of images. Of women getting up early, pre-dawn, as it was pre-dawn where I was on the ocean. They were heating the water to make the tsangpa, or the coffee, or the tea, or whatever their children or husbands needed to start the day. I felt that I was one with them and that there was a kind of sisterhood that I was part of. I felt honored and grateful to be allowed in.

Atlantic Voyage Journal

11/17/90 – Saturday

Land in Gran Canaria at 4:15 a.m. Catch bus into town (10-15 miles). Docks filled with perhaps 120 boats, all signed up for the Atlantic Rallye for Cruisers (ARC) from Gran Canaria to St. Lucia. Hang around, ask questions, be tired. Get a little depressed after asking 200 people and getting tight smiles and pleasant "No thank yous."

There are 30 notices up from 22-year-olds wanting to crew...AH SHIT! Does not look good. Big ARC rally. Only 150 boats to St. Lucia on 11/25 and they've almost all got set crew.

Start wondering if I want to jam into a little tube for up to a month and live cheek and jowl with three to four strangers. Now? No! Rather be on my own boat with Pat on the Islands. Hope the ocean is beautiful if I actually get on it.

Feel exhausted but body okay. Nothing to do but go back to the docks and keep asking. Have already asked some people two or three times. Depressed when I saw the slim chance. . .Todo es en los manos de Dios!

Feels like an exercise in absurdity if I don't get a ride. Today only first day. . .40 or so more boats expected before next Sunday. . .Universe will provide a boat or airfare back home if no boat.

11/18/90 – Sunday

Sitting on foredeck of Easy Easy, a 50-foot steel cutter built in a Yorkshire shipyard for Ed and Bill, two Englishmen in their 40s who've decided to give me a berth.

Had slept until about 10 a.m. . .shower, breakfast at local bar, then off to docks to ply my trade. Got a no from the only two possibilities left from yesterday. Spent another hour or so asking the same people. Called to a big soft burly man on a somewhat grotty looking steel boat. He spoke with me and said to come back in two hours, his partner was asleep. . .I returned and was taken on after about ten minutes.

The fourth man, a friend of theirs, is due today or tomorrow. Then we start putting it and ourselves together for Sunday's start. I have a couple of days before we start painting on Wednesday.

Will go to a few seminars that have been arranged, and by bus to another port on the island. I feel so well provided for. I asked why they took me – the answer, "Oh just a feeling." Who knows what this marriage will be for the four of us. The fourth guy, Ross, has no experience. So I'm the third of four and I hope I don't drown us. First Trans Atlantic sail for all of us.

Glad to have a ride. Want to leave tomorrow. Glad to be alive. . .Thank you God for most this amazing day. Goodnight my love (Pat Rodegast, his second wife). I'm off to sleep. Patty, I miss you.

My God, where am I? -- Las Canarias on a boat waiting to cross the ocean. . .Oh lordy me! Oh yes, the EPIRB sealed the deal (an old Garmin series 122 satellite navigation instrument). They needed one and I had one and all's well. Moved onto the boat at about 4 p.m. this afternoon.

11/20/90 – Tuesday

Fourth man – 36-year-old bull named Ross. . .policeman from Wakefield. He and Bill up to their ears in bilges. Went to a few seminars today. Then Bill, Ross, Ed and I spent four hours in the bowels of the beast trying to fix a stuffing box leak. At one point we were all jammed down into this horror show steel bilge. A wonderful peace came over me even though I was bailing in the bilge full of foul greasy diesel sea water. . .and losing ground. The seal seemed beyond fixing, we're taking on water and I see the voyage being shit-canned and the boat being hauled and fixed. . .a two-week job.

This going on and none of us is saying what we're feeling. I stop for a minute, put my hands up, close my eyes and smile. Maharaji is there. I am full of such peace and bliss. I smile and know that he has fixed the leak. Regardless of what happens next, he has fixed this. Ed is watching me although I try to mask my bliss and pleasure.

I smile and say, "I'll tell you on a watch," a phrase he has used with me meaning that there's some long story to relate. Bill and Ross make a pairing and Ed and I seem to.

They all smoke and drink a lot of beer so I will probably spend a lot of time here next to the mast, writing, sitting, praying and listening.

Eh Ram, Om Hari Om. Thank you God for most this exhausting day.

11/21/90 – Wednesday

Went up the mast today to check the rigging, lights, change a bulb. Scared a little, then faith – masthead is 80 feet over the water. Problem. . .I sleep in a bunk extending off the salon. Three chain smokers! They are asleep in the smoke. . .I can't breathe and so I go above deck. During the day, no problem. At night (12 p.m.) it is a problem. Also the smoke gathers in the room after they've gone to bed, I breathe it in. I have to present this to them and deal with it. I can't/won't do this for three weeks! I would have to get off the boat instead. My eyes and throat are sore now as I write.

11/22/90 – Thursday

Happy Birthday! My 50th. Last night Bill brought John from the boat next door onboard and it went on and on and on until 2:30 a.m. Very knowledgeable guy. Up at 8 a.m. We fueled up – partial comedy!

I made three too big salads for Thanksgiving gathering of about 40 people. . .nice time.

Anxious to go. Pat, the disorder and mess makes me crazy! I'm the neatnik. Another young Englishman comes on the boat tomorrow. Giles will probably trade carpentry for his food on the passage.

After dinner. . . 10 p.m. . .they all started to smoke and I just blurted out about my breathing and how I couldn't stay and be a passive smoker if they smoked in the salon at night. Some growling, hmmming. Me silent other than saying "I don't want to get between you and your cigarettes." Bill didn't want anyone "telling him he couldn't smoke." I said almost nothing. . .

After about 15 minutes, Bill and Ed struggled to "No Cigarettes on the Voyage!" Ed will do two cigars a day, but nothing below decks. Ross said he appreciated how hard it was to say what I did and especially before we set sail since the three could have said "Fuck you, get off the boat." I said I had to accept the fact that I might not be able to go because of the smoking.

At some point, each thanked me because they had vaguely intended to quit smoking and that this gave them a push.

I had been scared to say it because the passage was at stake, but I really wasn't going to live in the smoke. All seems okay until the withdrawals start. We sail Sunday noon. By Monday a.m.

there may be some shit to deal with since they'll smoke until Sunday noon.

11/23/90 – Friday

Day spent provisioning. . .Ross and I go to El Corte Ingles. . .enormous department store and supermercado – back to boat – back to Corte Ingles. We spent 87,500 pesetas ($875) on food. . .five of us. . .hours in the underground supermercado! Paying with cards and some cash.

At open air bar at the end of the pier, partially hunchback man works from 7 a.m. until 12 p.m. . .just does it. Also Don Pedro who runs the gas dock. . .beautiful. . .twinkle. He gets everyone in and out with much fuel, play and skill. Also hard working skinny young kid at counter next to smaller supermercado. . .beautiful in sad animal furtive-eyed way.

11/24/90 – Saturday

More provisioning, getting it together finally. Now the sail begins to be real. So many things that can't be done. Hope to paint decks with sand paint before we go. Very slippery when wet.

Went out for last meal ashore. Ed got "fair proper pissed" out of his mind. He was long gone out there to a scary place. . .in a waking trance of some sort. Me to bed at three, up at seven. They were even later.

11/25/90 – Sunday – Day 1

We are on our way. Almost the last ones out due to late phone calls. Just as well. We came up through some of the slower boats until they went off chasing the winds.

Exciting to start and begin to wrestle with this 30-ton beast. Took all of us to get it going. Rhythms all out of synch. Sailing wing on wing we were like a locomotive – strong, steady, tracking well – preventer on the main and spinnaker pole on the enormous genny.

The wind died down after a couple of hours. Bill said, "I bought the damn motor to use, let's turn it on. If I can't go five knots within 15 degrees of where I want, on goes the motor."

Now 6 a.m. on Monday. . .just finished the 3-6 a.m. watch with Giles. Haven't really slept. . .but I think now it's time. . .Scopalamine patch and wrist bands on. . .no illness so far!

Connecting with the hunchback, mi hermano, and Don Pedro made me cry with appreciation. Thank you God for most this amazing day!

Michael happy in his yacht's rigging, 1990

11/26/90 – Monday – Day 2

Still just getting used to boat and each other. Ross feeling punky. He has some sea bands and just put them on. I'm fine. Sleep all messed up and slightly constipated.

Motoring through deep swells is a drag. We have them on the beam so there is much pitching up and down. My bunk is about two feet from the uninsulated door to the diesel. . .a little like the seaplane from St. Croix to St. Thomas.

Everything still clumsy. It'll be okay. Bill is a fraud. . .presents himself as a bit of a buffoon but is no fool.

11/27/90 – Tuesday – Day 3

Ross' seasickness abating. . .then he got sunburned!

On totally open undulating field of blue. Swells were choppy the first few days, now long soft easy. Very gentle although massive. Some were 100 yards across.

Winds too light for such a heavy boat. Been motoring 80% of the time, just waiting for steady ten knot and over winds. There is much to do to get boat really together. We're all still just getting acclimatized. . .its been aboard 53 hours. It takes some time but, we're all doing well. Motor has been on 43 of the 53 hours!

Have done little sitting so far but it will come. Must find a place that's secure in the pitching and rolling.

11/28/90 – Wednesday – Day 4

Still on the motor. . .slow, noisy, stinky. All getting mildly impatient. No showers until 500 miles in order to save water. We are all dirty and disappointed with motoring. No disaster, but it will all take longer. Probably not home by the 20th.

Slept about eight hours. No seasickness. I'm fine.

Hard to get a quiet place/time to meditate. Sitting forward of the mast I need a harness or I'll fall overboard.

The mind sets up models – I have been waiting. . .looking for some specialness so that I can hear/see Emmanuel and Maharaji. . .expectation of some magic form.

Rearranged the fruits and vegetables. I had the 6-9 watch both a.m. and p.m. Bill caught a fish. I had a thimbleful. It tasted nice but no, no killing in order to feed me. . .I begin a soft fast tomorrow.

11/29/90 – Thursday – Day 5

My watch 9-12 a.m. and p.m. . .10 a.m. now. . .maybe some lightly building wind. We've motored 86 of 96 hours! Longing for the noise and vibration to stop. Feels like boat is a patient etherized upon a table while the motoring operation goes on.

I am bored with my own seeking of "enlightenment." There's this "holiness evaluator" who judges everything I do on the scale of – "Will this/that thought/word/deed bring me closer to enlightenment/perfection?"

Very dualistic (good/bad – right/wrong) and very judgmental. . . "make the smallest distinction however, and heaven and earth are set infinitely apart."

Pathetic, it's pathetic. . .and yet and yet. There is, in a sense, nothing else to do. For now, it is merely to soften. "And this too and this too." At times like this, my heart would/does break for all of our hunger and striving for home, the sweetness of home.

Something different starting now on the 9-noon watch. Sitting cross-legged at the helm in just my underpants. . .feels good. . . so simple.

Michael meditating at the mast

350 miles SW of Canaries towards the Cape Verdes. With two knots of wind, Giles is holding the jib clew over the rail so it doesn't flog on the stay. A bit futile. . .probably need to pole it out.

11/30/90 – Friday – Day 6

No watch, just cooking today. The driving noise and vibration of the Perkins diesel is deadening, draining! Four and a half days of diesel vibe!

The ocean is a fluctuation of vast blue. Can see boats six to seven miles in each direction. We float in the middle with no sense of progress or movement. Other boats so far away they disappear ahead, abeam, abaft, whatever.

We are so paltry in the midst of this. Someone asked Trungpa Rinpoche what it all felt like to him. He said, "I'm a piece of dust in an international jet airport." I'm beginning to understand.

Mind can't get around it, only as an idea, not the experience. As above, there's a circle of probably 12 to 15 miles diameter that is real experience, the rest is just more of the same through time. . . a concept.

Nothing happens anywhere else. . .only here – in this boat, at this time, in this place. It all may. . . does. . .change, but I'm still here, no where else, no when else. . .All the rest is empty ideas.

Bill and Ed almost dangerously dis/unorganized. Things happen impulsively. . .sails up, sails down. No drill, no procedure. We've had no agreement, discussion. . .whoever, whatever, wherever, whenever. We go until there's a problem. . .We deal with it then the next problem. . .a series of jerky jumps. . .lurching forward.

The masthead is 87 feet above the water, 75 feet from the cabin top. The boom is 28 feet long. I hate the boom. It is such a massive heavy thing. I deal with it like a hostile dog. I stay very careful with/ of/toward/about it. The boom is how we could be hurt badly.

Giles is also very careful because of Bill and Ed's untogetherness. They are both semi-controlled alcoholics. Although Ed and Bill don't see a need for a preventer when jibing, Giles and I make sure there's always one on the boom. Is this trip ever a mixed bag. Too much is left to chance. Too untogether on the boat. We will get there alive, but not due to our preparation. Planning is essentially spur of the moment.

So what! Fuck it, I'm here. I just wish we could get out of the noise of the motor. Goodnight love. Now 0:45, off to bed.

12/1/90 – Saturday – Day 7

Made pasta with mucho garlic and onion in tomato sauce! Ate too much of course. So good. Too much work though. . .whatever.

Took shower this a.m. Oh God, seven days without a shower is too long. Petty irritations starting to build in me. Judging Ed's being so decadent and Ross' rock and roll having to be played so loud. He's like a loyal bull dog who's a bit lost on this weird voyage. Bugged at Bill for not being a better and more organized skipper. Obviously I wanted him to take me in tow and teach me more. Oh well.

I want some quiet and I'm sure not getting any. That bleeping motor!

Going on a 202 degree heading which will take us too far south, towards the Cape Verdes. We should be on a 240 heading going further west. Bill wants to keep the jib full so that he thinks he's sailing. Big mistake! My vast experience speaks.

Leaning against the mast in the shade. Soft breeze in my face. . .eight-foot swells a quarter mile apart. . .long soft and streaky clouds up high. Without my irritations, this is exquisite. When will I stop being distracted by stuff around me?. . .distracted from saying yes to the perfection. . .so much attachment to right/wrong.

My fear is that we will be too far south and go through the band of the trades. If so, we're then in the middle of somewhere without enough fuel to drive and no real sense of where to go.

The struggle I go through is whether to make a pain in the ass of myself and insist when I don't know any better than anyone else, or just let it go. There is some "if we mess up, it's your fault, Bill" in it.

Just spoke my piece about direction. Giles independently verified it. Some vague "compromise" struck. It will all be well. When moving without anger, movement is possible. It is all going to be what it is anyway since everyone's "karma" has to be satisfied. So, never worry, not in danger. Only task is to soften around one's fear, then speak, move gently and clearly. Others will hear as best they can.

I absolutely appreciate having the privacy of the quarter berth even though it's open. . .I have it to myself.

Bill insistently and absolutely commits himself to a course of action. . .and then changes it 20 minutes later . . .oh well. . .I have the 3-6 a.m. watch, so off to bed.

Up again at 10:30 p.m. to tack the main sail across, jibe the jib, set the preventer, tie off the running back stay. . .love sailing on a full moon night with wind too close on the nose, Bill happy on the helm and thank you God!

12/2/90 – Sunday – Day 8

Somewhere near Latitude 19N and Longitude 23W, north of the Cape Verde Islands. At 10 a.m., a cargo vessel out of Nigeria, heading for England, reports the trade winds are another 200 to 300 miles farther!

We've come about 750 so far, nearly all on the motor. So we continue heading at 240 degrees which is what we were originally told to do. . .onward.

We have tried all kinds of crap and gone all over the place to end up back on the original heading. . .much boredom, hope, excitement and some worry. This has so far been a voyage of surrender.

Satellite Navigation is a jewel. It said we were 70 nautical miles off point of Cape Verdes. . .and there dead ahead, way off, the Cape Verdes. It is now 13:00 hours. We will get there at 23:00-24:00 hours – and stay long enough to get more diesel. More excitement since we might well crash into something!

Bill is almost out of control. He gets all heated up, worried, obsesses and does everything by himself. It's all pretty simple and straight forward but he's almost incapable of asking for help. For fear perhaps he won't look like the big strong bluster boy he masks. I say soothing things. Ed stands on the side, then comes in to do something impulsive. Oh shit!

Everyone got caught up in Bill's fear about where we were. I knew we were okay and said so, but BIll couldn't hear it. Finally it evolved so that it was clear that what I told him was true.

With all this, Bill, whose job dinner was, hadn't made any food. Everyone stood around – so I volunteered to make soup – two packs of Knorr's and a can of lentils. They all think they'll die if they don't have meat. . .so someone said, "corned beef sandwiches." I opened a tin and started to laugh. The grease was congealed and it looked and smelled like dog food.

There were no clean plates because no one had done the dishes. (Bill's job.) No one offered to help. . .no one was around. They are little boys fed first by Mommy and then waitresses or wives. . .sad. The whole two weeks of non-stop beer, meat and smoking got to me and I started feeling my irritation at their dumb, impulsive, smug piggishness. A wave of disgust came over me like a fever. It lasted only a few minutes and now it's over.

There is a quiet resolve in me for just doing – not engaging with them so close. Don't know.

Now about 10 p.m. . .the melodrama will start in about an hour. . .getting to dock at Sao Vicente, Cape Verde Islands.

I want to be seen and appreciated for my skill, judgment and contribution in an invisible sort of way. . .a problem for me, a historical problem. I want my brothers to see and appreciate me.

Entering harbor – Bill and Ed unable/unwilling to call on radio to get directions from ARC boats already in the harbor. Bill ditzing around to get SatNav perfect which it isn't. We sit around for two hours when 15 minutes of driving past the next headlands would have unveiled the port! Bill is, behind his 6' 6" 280 pound Barnacle Bill exterior, frightened and doubtful, harassed in his own head. He's very anxious, outloud, stubbornly, insistently. Ed is absolutely dishonest and duplicitous behind a decadent little boy charm, with a stinking cigar in his mouth.

Got into Cape Verdes at 2 a.m.

12/3/90 – Monday – Day 9

A 32-year-old American named Keith rafted up with us at about 10 a.m. He's just finishing a single handed circumnavigation over a four-year period. On way home to Virginia. He's going home to make money, get a 50' racing trimaran and take people on charter "white knuckles" portions of his next circumnavigation. . .at $60/day. . .good adventure.

Anyway, within ten minutes of his tying up next to us I asked him to take me with him. He smiled, recognized and commiserated. . .he was just doing single-handed. His suggestion was to pick up whatever seamanship I could while I was in this. . .will do. This stop demarcates. We have probably two and a half more weeks and I will just teach myself whatever I can. Just hanging out in Sao Vicente harbor until about 4 p.m. when we get fuel. Hopefully we leave tomorrow.

12/4/90 – Tuesday – Day 10

Finally fueled. . .we leave at 14:45 into a strong wind in the right direction aiming us towards the Caribbean. Had seen a weatherfax that said no real wind. We get out of the harbor into 20 knots! We come up into the wind and put out the genoa on a pole and put the main out with a preventer off the port bow. (Preventer is a heavy line with a bowline knot on the aft end of the boom and runs outside through the port fairlead to a heavy cleat at the bow.)

Bill takes the helm for an hour then tells Ross to take it. . .We have ten foot following seas and Ross has never had the helm before. Bill sits behind and Ross is learning. After a while, we are below and the boat starts going strongly off to port and heeling like crazy. I look up the companionway and there is Ross terrified and fighting the wheel. He is almost crying in this terror. A gust had come up, turned the stern a little and he had overcorrected in the wrong direction.

The result was that the wind was now too far over to port, and had back filled the main from the port beam. Thank God for the preventer or an enormous 75-foot high, 28-foot long main sail on the biggest boom I will ever have sailed with (our own Toy Boat's mast is 30-feet high and this boom is easily five to seven times as heavy). . .would have accidentally gibed at head height and killed him and perhaps have taken the mast too! This in the first one and a half hours!

We were overpowered but big dumb-assed Bill says we'll be okay! He's 6' 6" and 280 pounds. I guess he likes power.

It is 21:30 as I write. I'm trying to sleep before my midnight to 4 a.m. watch but I can't. I'm scared. The trip from Canaria to here was almost all by motor which has an awful security to it. . .nothing could break or go wrong but the engine. . .now we could get into trouble with our sails!

I remember Emmanuel and Maharaji and it helps. Fear is there and it will just go through me in however long it takes, but it is here now. We are really out in the middle of the bleeping ocean with 2,000 !!!!!!! miles to go. I am scared. . .this too shall pass, I hope. Lo mano de Dios.

My fear will come and calm will come and fear will come and calm – Oh Lordy be! Thank you God for most this amazing day.

I cannot tell you how sad Cape Verde is. The worst, worst, worst of Tijuana with no stores, no stuff, nothing. Third world poverty. Heavy. . .I walked through the streets feeling some of the overwhelming pain for suffering I felt in India. Everyone in America should see it and live in it for a while, and then maybe stop complaining about manufactured pains, empty desires based on greed and fear. I can't get around it to see the perfection yet. The pain gets me too personally.

Can't sleep. Am up at 23:45. The wind has calmed down a bit. We've come down from making 9.4 knots to 4.5 It was all a bit much with heavy wind, choppy seas and us going two knots over maximum hull speed. . .It's midnight and I go on four hours watch.

12/5/90 – Wednesday – Day 11

Dolphins at dusk! About 15 of them swimming off the bow. They came about an hour after I made tuna sandwiches for everyone, including myself. I guess they came to remind me that I can't really just go ahead and pretend that I can mindlessly eat tuna fish. . .or sheep or people or any of the rest of the bloody carnivorous living things.

Going on watch 20:00 to 24:00 – ocean is big – this is bloody dangerous – don't need blinding speed of a faster boat! More anon. Too tired to write more.

12/6/90 – Thursday – Day 12

Ed let me sleep in for two extra hours. I got seven hours of sleep! Perfect timing! Thank you God. Now I'm letting Giles sleep extra. Good to be alone in the cockpit at 7 a.m. with no talk, no music, no cigars, no beer.

Giles just got up, but he and I don't talk so it's fine.

At 8 a.m. we had gone 203 miles from Cape Verde. . .averaging five knots. . .1,800 to go!

Aah the ocean. . .My favorite is the big rolling waves. Big undulating mountains of water rolling under us. . .picking us up to the heights. . .maybe an extra 20 feet. . .the vista. . .endless water. . .perhaps an additional ten miles view over the normal five-mile visibility. . .then, past the crest, the descent begins, past the spring-summer-autumn to the depths of January, February.

At the bottom, one can see perhaps a half mile down a narrow canyon of water. There is no promise, no expansion, only limited circumstances. . .like the Nigerians, Ghanaians and Liberians back at Cape Verde. Not being able to go forward or back. . .unwanted, unable to move.

Michael holding the jib

Then the beginning of the next rise. . .I love it. . .Lazarus rising again from the dead. . .the covenant apparently still in force. . .(If we don't totally freak and do something overwhelmingly stupid, God will keep us going.)

I also love the predictability of the movement of the rollers. Had rough chop yesterday. . .big cross chop against the main rollers. Big pointed chunks of water banging into each other, creating a sub chop. The boat bounces around in no predictable manner. Confused seas is the phrase for it and it's a good one. We were dealing with bouncing around in 15-foot seas with maybe 18 to 20 knot winds. . .I don't ever want to see boiling seas at 40 to 50 knots!

The fact that the boat floats is a loving miracle.

I have slept, eating is under control (will be eating very lightly), no more coffee or tea out of boredom, shaving every five days, have shit, not sunburned (being careful). . .I'm beginning to feel lean again. . .all is well. It's almost impossible to stay really clean since we have water for showers only every 500 miles.

Almost impossible to meditate. Too much movement and noise. Just sat for a few minutes. Not so easy. Body doing constant adjustment to the pitching and rolling of the boat.

Last night when the dolphins were at the bow, I sat at the mast and did my overtone chanting towards them and it soothed me in a way that was such a gift. This voyage has been an almost non-stop ordeal for me so far. . .except for a few moments of bliss. . .not a bad trade-off.

I think I love sailing. . .with some conditions. . .manageable sails. . .clean people. . .procedures worked out beforehand. . .no one sails a boat alone. . .Giles, 26-year-old recent graduate of some British sailing school, runs around sailing the boat alone. So does Bill, but BIG!!!, and, in his own passive aggressive way, so does Ed – oh Lordy be! Ross drinks.

The four of them seem to be in some sort of eating contest. . .men are strong, work hard, drink, smoke, swear, and eat a lot. . .BIG BOYS. . .We are running out of food in about five days and we have 15 to go. A boat needs food discipline on any sort of passage. This one doesn't until Bill sees the reality.

We brought on ten large and ten small loaves of good bread from Cape Verde. Bill and Giles each ate a large loaf with tuna for lunch yesterday joking about how hungry big men get. . .BIG BOYS.

There are 20 major little things that need to be fixed. One is the compass light. We can't hand steer at night because we can't read the compass. There's a SATNAV compass but it is too far from the helm to read. If the autohelm goes we are in deep shit, deeply so on a very big deep ocean.

That's just one thing. On a boat, if it's wrong, it has to be fixed. . .NOW. . .because of the Law of Dominoes (one thing leads to another). . .a small thing wrong can become a big danger very quick.

Have to know where everything is. This is so disorganized that no one knows where anything is. . .so, every time something is needed, the whole boat gets searched. . .always Marx Brothers routines. I am so glad this is not a hard weather crossing or it would really be dangerous. When we land, I will get off and never get on this boat again.

Bill resents Ed (for pretty good reason) so he mumbles and grumbles. Ed is cuter. . .he does his grumbling more surreptitiously. The result undermines teamwork of course, quiet, below the surface, but there. . .ready to erupt at God knows what moment. Personal stuff has to be straightened out somehow.

I am in fact learning a great deal. I am sure there will be more. I have learned much more about seamanship than about sailing as such. That's okay I can see now. The sailing will come and it's probably not all that complicated. The issues of discipline and integrity and the like are the underlying issues that define sailing skill more than factual knowledge and expertise.

Ed let me sleep. I let Giles sleep. We need to help each other. The five of us are spaced out all over the boat. . .it's great.

In many ways the trip has been profoundly disappointing. The boat, the wind, the men. It has felt more like an ordeal than any kind of pleasure cruise. And when I was frightened a few days ago, I thought I had designed hell for myself.

All Giles' running around will add maybe 39 to 50 miles of speed over 2,700 miles. . .negligible. More together human beings would create a difference in quality of life which would add immeasurably to safety and comfort on an enormous scale and that defines success in a way that going faster can't.

Valuable, however unpleasant, a passage. My inability to change boats was probably in some ways for the best, although I personally hate being where I am.

Shaved earlier. . .feels so good. Started to lose some weight. I would love to fast now but won't due to the stresses that already exist. Also, I need strength reserves. However, I was offered food earlier and asked my body first if it wanted food. . .no hunger, no need, no thank you. . .free of eating out of boredom and fear. Have been taking vitamins, will start drinking instant miso soup to insure a base of some protein. Also, I asked to take two small rounds of cheese with individual portions to be mine, as protein, since I have paid for and won't eat any of the meat and fish.

12/7/90 – Friday – Day 13

Last night I had a good quiet time up on the cockpit roof leaning against the furled main. Very meditative space. I have just a few techniques for getting quiet and open hearted – and thank God I do have them. I feel fine. In a groove. Before, Bill was real grumpy above decks. When I saw him, my own gladness lifted him and for the nonce he's okay. I wish my judging mind would shut off more than it does, but that's okay too.

I don't know if I want to cross the ocean again, but I sure want to sail with you – some goodly voyages.

I have so much more respect for the simplicity of Jack's boat. . .solar electric, outboard motor – oh glory be! There's a Newick clone shell in Wales. I will call about it.

The wooden ring swelled and cracked so now it is on my large finger. I use it as a reminder of you. We are so precious to each other, you and I, and I am so ashamed of my ill humours.

I find myself saying to Giles often under my breath, "To be correct and to be right are not the same thing." It would be well if I could remember that myself upon more occasions. . .I do have moments of having no opinions about anything and I love it.

It's now 14:00 hours on the third day out of Cape Verde. We're 350 miles out – approximately 1,700 to go! At 120 miles/day = 14 to 15 days more! ETA now December 22 – oh shit. I promised you to be back by Dec. 20.

We have been going further south chasing the mythical trade winds which we were supposed to hit 100 miles out of Gran Canaria. . .just no wind!. . .happens sometimes. . .but no one talks about it.

On one level this has been "an insufferable hell". . .and yet and yet. . .have faith. If what Emmanuel and Maharaji say is true, it's all written by our souls. . .just keep on keeping on!

At dinner I said, "Okay, when the hell are we turning west?" Everyone is afraid of Bill who still thinks we have to go further south. He just can't accept that this year it just ain't the way the books say it's supposed to be. After much hemming and hawing, he said, "We'll see when we hit 12 degrees 30 minutes". . .I have the 3 to 6 a.m. watch so I'm off to try to sleep.

Giles just heard something on the radio saying that there is more wind to the west. An hour earlier I had been arguing to go west, but Ed and Bill insisted on going south. Because of this latest report we abruptly turned 20 degrees further west. When I asked Bill what happened, he mumbled something to the effect that we couldn't hear all the message but we turned 20 degrees west none-theless. This trip is requiring much faith from me.

My position here is that I'm a little weird (vegetarian, no beer, no smoking) and since I don't act like a BIG BOY, I can't know anything. So, I'm pretty much ignored unless I say it strongly. But I don't do that much any more. . .too much struggle.

Neither Ed nor Bill has any self discipline. Giles is a self important "handsomeyoungman" who knows everything and covers the rest with strong opinion. . .He's 26. . .Ross is the young bull policeman (36) body builder, rugby player, drinking partner who's actually the most trustworthy of the bunch.

It's good for me, this. I get to see them and me in our/my own trips. But I don't like it. I love the ocean and will miss it, but I can't wait to get off this beast!

12/8/90 – Saturday – Day 14

Earlier on my 3:30 to 7 a.m. watch, we passed below 12 degrees 30 minutes. It was with much delight that Ross and I turned the AutoHelm up to 284 degrees which aimed us due True West! Having gone below St. Lucia going SW was starting to take us further away, rather than closer. Also, at about 6 a.m. the wind started to pick up. I think finally at 12 degrees 16 minutes north, 31 degrees and 39 minutes west we have begun to get the trade winds! We now have 1,770 miles to go. At least we are no longer chasing Bill's insistence that we go south to catch the trades.

It is clear that I was the badger to get Bill to agree to go west. The fact that we got the winds so soon after was Lo Mano de Dios. It took courage on my part. Now I am good to have on board.

Now, of course, I don't want the wind to go above 13 to 15 knots or to shift at all. Bill expects us all to be absolutely knowledgeable and then treats us as though we were ninnies. . .oh well, not always taking it personally. He and I can joke with each other a little now. He called me a "whining c__t." I smiled and said I'd tell "me mum" on him and that he was lucky to have me on board. . .and it's true.

None of the four of them know anything about food. For them it is sex, safety, BIG BOY competition and some football macho BULLSHIT. . .(no judgments on my part of course). I am so tired of the sight and smell of them gorging on burnt dead pigs!

We are now doing one hour each on the helm. We are undoubtedly over-powered with the full main on a starboard broad reach, but will not reel down until past the point of clear danger. Bill is now at the helm and is clearly struggling but will/cannot admit it. . .So tiresome, this whole thing. Before, when I was really angry, my heart was closed to them. It isn't now, but I will not walk another step with any of them once we hit St. Lucia. Ed and Bill are crude and dishonest and without much integrity.

Giles doesn't know correct from right yet – and being healthy and attractive should keep him trapped for quite a while.

Ross is like a loyal dog who growls when needed and is happy when given a good meat bone to chew. He's the best of the bunch although willfully stupid in his actions.

Two more weeks if I'm lucky. God, bless the AutoHelm SATNAV, engine, food and moderate wind!. . .this is a textbook case of how not to sail.

I just glanced at the big new yellow horseshoe (man overboard float) that mounts on the pushpit (aft rail, like the pulpit forward). It's been there, under the chart table for God knows how long. I just decided to put it where it belongs. I asked Ed why it wasn't up and he said something about a backing plate, I just tied it with some cord. When I put the plastic wrapper away, it said CREWSAVER on it!

Just made pasta for dinner. Tomato and a can of dogfood-type corned beef for them and garlic, onions and oil for me. I made sure there was a small bottle of olive oil on board.

12/9/90 – Sunday – Day 15

11 a.m. Just took a bucket bath and shaved. Feels good. Down at latitude 12 degrees, 03 minutes, longitude 35 west. Only 720 miles north of the Equator! 1,800 nm south of NYC. We are at the same latitude as the coast of Venezuela, Honduras, Guatemala, Gambia, Guinea-Bissau, Mauritania in Africa.

Sprouts coming up good. We'll have them every other day until they run out. I'll make small amounts or the BIG BOYS will wolf them down. Their mindless eating is overwhelming. Giles and Bill being the worst.

The ocean is so beautiful! I take a few pictures but they don't capture the rhythm. The beauty is in the rhythm. Whether the long slow rollers I love or light chop or big chop, it's the rhythm.

The water's coming off the starboard quarter so it throws the boat around a bit making the helm hard work. I've gotten pretty good at it but it sure is hard on this boat. . .Harder than the Morgan Beneteau or O'Day. . .60,000 pounds!. . .my Toy Boat weights 1,600!

I have developed so much respect for the ocean and being on it. . .Not to be taken lightly. I have a low level apprehension about the wind switching around us. We are sailing wing on wing. . .Main to port with a line from the bow to the aft end of the boom as a preventer and the big jib out with the spinnaker pole to starboard. The problem could be the need to take in or drop sail quickly, which we can't do. Probably would take 30 minutes because of the size, weight and therefore complexity of dropping them.

This is a vulnerability I don't enjoy. Being overpowered is a risk of time as well as size and wind.

As my fear (concern) comes up, I move to faith. Part of it is faith that Maharaji and Emmanuel said I'd make it home. . .simply that my Good Fairies will indeed protect me as they said they would.

But there is another one I've been finding that is very far out. Our souls have independently and collectively chosen to set this in motion for purposes known only outside and beyond our intellects and personalities. Whatever happens is not an accident, but purposeful in the most loving way to bring us closer to truth, wisdom and simply being, in whatever form.

We are, as it were, always in the hands and sight of God, as formed by our individual souls using the forms and medium of Earth, body, mind. This growing knowing gives me much peace and a sense of tender sweetness – a much broader and softer gaze toward the world within which we sail.

I deeply dislike my company. I will or won't make NYC by the 20th. You will or will not love me as much as before. I will drown out here, or whatever fear conjures up, or even love conjures. Making love with you, being silly giggling and gilly siggling together, taking your and my grandchildren sailing and playing.

All is held in a soft, softer gaze with the Buddha's smile of infinite compassion. It's okay, Michael Projansky can resent the irresponsible boorishness of these four guys. It's understood and expected as part of Disney World.

I wish I could just really tell this to you in an instant mind – grok instead of scribbling clumsily on a lurching pig of a boat. . .Oh well. I know I'll be back by the time you read this (or dead and therefore never read) but please tell Emmanuel and Maharaji that I've been hearing some interesting subtle things, even if I don't hear and see them in clear words and forms. But I did see Maharaji put his hand on Bill when we were fixing the leaking bearing sleeve. For sure!

I love your fish eyeglass case. . .I love you. . .bigger than the ocean and that is a whole lot of big. . .whoooooooooeeee yess'm.

Part of what I started out to say a page ago is that as fear creates images of smashing booms, masts and drowning, after the rush of fear in the body, there is also a sense of okayness. . .a willingness to go with it, whatever it is – to move with the rhythm rather than the usual mind's attempt to dictate everything. . .poor mind.

In Zorba the Greek, Zorba says very lovingly of women ". . .they are such poor weak creatures and they give you everything they got. . ." Poor mind, it is such a poor weak creature and it tries to control everything it's got. . .

Just thinking about the young people in my life. . .I was just holding them all so tenderly. . .my girls, your boys in Monroe and in Florida. . .

12/10/90 – Monday – Day 16

Realized earlier, sitting next to Bill in the cockpit that I had given him the nickname of the Bear. He actually looks like one. I remembered the story of you and me being told by Emmanuel and

Maharaji that they would send a bear to chase us away if we ever got into a dangerous situation. . .well, here I am in this frigging lair!. . .so much for my being a good judge of character or a good student!. . .for this a PhD in Psych no less!

Main sail goes up before dinner. . .okay! Wind strong – another dangerous sail change with Bill half drunk. . .not only impulsive, but stupid too. There was a gleeful crazed look in his eyes that certain drunks get. . .a wild intoxication. . .where drink frees them from bonds and they touch exhilaration and no limits. . .freedom! It's great on the dance floor, but almost criminal in its stupidity on a boat 1,400 miles from the nearest port.

I stood at the aft end of the boom and told myself, "Be careful, don't get injured. Let the boat break, but don't you break."

Giles has his own madness. He can't stand the fact that anyone else is on the boat. Because he's actually the most knowledgeable, he's the de facto captain, but he runs around trying to do every job. . .At one point he was in the cockpit trying to do three things at once while I was standing there ready to help. I had to yell at him that I had one of the lines and was doing it myself.

When the vang broke (too small for the rig since Bill and Ed didn't think they could afford the rig the architect designed), I ended up helming for about one and a half hours in very heavy wind (30 knots) and very heavy seas (15 to 18 feet). . .tired boy this one.

Now 1:30 a.m. and I'm on at 3:30 a.m. Can't sleep because of the rock and roll. . .have to try. . .Hope I live through this.

12/11/90 – Tuesday – Day 17

What a wild ride. Toughest weather yet. Hope it's not the coming attractions. No sleep at all prior to my 3:00 to 6:30 a.m. watch. My watch was hard and beautiful. . .the wind was strong, 25 to 30 mph and the seas were big. The moon was hidden behind clouds so we were just flying in the dark.

Ed couldn't sleep so he was in and out, up and down. I wanted to be alone but it was okay. . .had to steer by hand for two and a half hours since the wind was ahead of the beam and shifting so I had to constantly adjust course so that we could use the wind. . .good practice.

15:00 hours. . .872 miles from Cape Verde, 1,642 from the beginning in the Canaries and 1,270 to go to St. Lucia. Won't make it by December 20. Sorry. I wanted to get to St. Lucia on December 20. . .catch a flight that a.m. and surprise you at Judith's, all healthy and tan and heroic and all. Instead I am left with gnawing worry until we get there the 21st or 22nd or whenever and I can call, having already been late. . .glub glub.

Feeling the edges of more freedom. Been obviously struggling with these guys. . .just realized that if I have no fear, the whole thing changes. Fear of their gluttony is that we'll run out of food. I can fast. I've already done it before for 12 days. . .Fear of their drunkenness is that we'll crash and burn and die. . .Emmanuel and Maharaji said it would be okay. . .also, if we do, then that was my soul's irrefutable perfect choice. . .no problem in that. . .their coarseness and dishonesty. . .the fear says that I'll have to be in this forever without any power to change it and I know that's not true. . .things will happen to change whatever this is into something else. . .

The whole thing is clear and obvious to anyone who isn't here because there they have no fear. . .but I have been in fear and so nothing was obvious or visible to the point where I have been blinded by my fear. . .hmmm.

I'm working with a bunch of aversions. . .Bill's drunkenness. . .he gets dangerously impulsive when he's drunk with almost no warning. It's only happened a few times so far, but it's really dangerous when he does.

So I was asking Emmanuel and Maharaji, "Do I have to put up with a drunk and dangerous captain?". . .Well, if there is no danger because I'm safe, we're all safe, then it is just stupid noise he's making and if I just stay clear and don't try to change or fix him all will be well. . .hard one for my demanding mind that says, "He's got no business being drunk on a boat."

And all the rest of it. We're either safe or we're not. . .There are either "karmic" mistakes or there aren't. . .Faith gets pretty crunchy and spiny some times. . .hmmmmm.

12/12/90 – Wednesday – Day 18

11:30 a.m. . .1,000 miles out of Cape Verde. 1,140 to go! Latitude 12 degrees and 14 minutes north, longitude 42 degrees and 11 minutes west.

Winds are off the starboard one quarter at anywhere from 20 to 30 mph tops! Very hard work when the winds are high and the seas build up big. The waves are sometimes up to 20 feet. . .Big and a bit scary because. . .if two waves in a row hit the wrong way, you're almost broadside at 30 degrees off course. So it takes complete concentration and a lot of strength. We are, I hope, at the maximum of winds and seas!

It's now 4 p.m. We'll have to put the third reef in the main and furl the jib in a bit if it keeps up this way. Hand steering at night will be a bitch since the compass binnacle light is broken. Boat's been bouncing so much that it's been hard to sleep the last three days. Never get fully asleep. . .so I'm in a strange kind of waking daze.

Bill just angrily announced that someone stuffed up the head. . .and, true to form, no one either used the head or knows how to fix it. So, I got a wire hanger and tried to break it up. Got my hands down into it. Everyone was horrified. What babies BIG BOYS are!. . .Haven't they ever changed and washed diapers?

Still working with yesterday's stuff about fear and aversion and me and them. Interesting issue of no "strong" preferences, or at least softening greatly my aversions once I see what the fear is that lies within me. . .then whatever lies in front of me can become dualistic and adversarial.

No need to fight ". . .every little thing gonna be alright. . ."

Compassion can only exist when there is great faith. Without faith, it is pity or posing or denial, something not quite clean. Compassion's not about someone else's misfortune or unfortunate circumstances. It can only be about us. . .me too. . .or it is smarmy in some subtle distancing way. . .boy, what a gift to be getting this one. . .I have to be living it or I'm just some spectator pretending to be involved. . .it has to be my hunger . . .I have to know that there is no real distance between thee and me. . .that's the issue. . .no difference between thee and me.

Wind much stronger now. We are flying along. I might make the party at Judith's. . .IF. . .1. The wind keeps up, 2. We clear in at St. Lucia quickly, and 3. I can get a flight. If I can make the party, I'll surprise you. If not, I'll call as soon as I can.

12/13/90 – Thursday – Day 19

Good sailing day. 947 miles to go! Latitude 12 degrees, 20 minutes north, longitude 45 degrees, 05 minutes west.

Two new knots from Giles – a double sheet bend. . .static joining of two lines. . .a dolly. . .a moving tightener knot. . .both are used as a preventer.

Ross – called him on using me as the casual butt of a stupid joke. . .It was about my helming (of which I happen to be pleased). I said, "Ross, I work hard at the helm and that (the joke) doesn't help." It stopped him.

There's an unconscious violating of everyone and everything. It's not good for anyone. . .only spreads doubt and paranoia. I won't let Ross do it because: 1. It hurts even if only a little; 2. It's not in truth; 3. I don't want to foster it by acquiescence (can't you take a joke?); and 4. The motivation behind it isn't clean. Let's you and I never do it again with each other. . .I vow to stop.

12/14/90 – Friday – Day 20

Course – 303 degrees west. . .2,089 miles from Gran Canaria – 759 to go.

Latitude 12 degrees, 04 minutes north, longitude 48 degrees, 14 minutes west.

I spent part of my watch last night with Maharaji. . .We were living together in a great big gunny sack of burlap in a side alley off the bazaar in some Arab or Indian town. . .many years ago. . .before cars or electricity.

Each morning we would get up and I would follow him. . .sometimes behind, sometimes next to him. . .we would go wherever he took me. . .he had things to do that I was to see. . .just gestures, a movement, an interaction. . .very simple. Each day brought its events and it seemed clear that there was no planning and arranging of any of it. . .it just happened. . .although I don't know whatever communications Maharaji might have had with the universe outside his apparent interactions with me.

The main thing was the doing/being wherever it was. . .the no big deal of it. . .and he was absolutely clear about whatever he was doing. . .nothing would have been able to stop him.

In the vision we had obviously been about this for some years, living very simply like this when one morning, he motioned for me to follow him. . .the sense was that we were going somewhere and there would be no talk or other activity until we got there.

We arrived at a place which was an opening under a bridge or an aqueduct. . .it was a stone vaulted space that was out of the way, out of the flow of traffic. There were about 15 people who were just hanging out together.

The focal point was a palette on which there lay what appeared to be a very old man. . .who wasn't quite a man. . .he had an androgynous quality about him. He was clearly so old, that he was an ancient. There was no human fleshiness about him. He was pared down to the minimum. . .he was apparently human. . .but probably more angel than human. . .an elder.

The feeling I had was that he was visiting in order to do some work. . .and we were there as part of that. . .although Maharaji hadn't indicated anything to me about it other than being very particular about getting there. However, when we got there, all of a sudden, Maharaji looked young, as though he were in his mid-50s and his demeanor towards this being was very much that of a younger man deferring to an elder. . .very respectful.

He blessed Maharaji and then I was motioned over to him. . .I had a sense that I was Maharaji's student and that I was now being presented for examination to see how well I was progressing. . .I was so glad to see that Maharaji was himself pleased with me. . .but he was clearly deferring to this being who he loved a great deal.

The examination consisted of my simply sitting before the elder. Prior to looking into his eyes, I saw him as being utterly old and ancient. . .one who was beyond caring, one who's compassion had nothing personal left. . .It was all beyond the personal investment in outcomes, whether for him or the other. . .there was only the inexorable working out of whatever was being worked out.

I looked into his eyes and could see only the vast night sky. There was no one there to look at. As I was simply looking at the sky deeply in wherever I was seeing, he must have been doing/seeing whatever it was that he was there to do/see. . .me, I suppose. . .but certainly not on any level I could know about or do anything about.

After some amount of time, he was apparently satisfied and the examination was finished. . .I had not had any particularly unusual experience but I knew that this was a very, very high being and that this was a very important thing that was happening.

I bowed to him and he looked at me with a tenderness that was neither warm nor cold, soft nor hard, but vast. . .I couldn't follow it back to where it had started from. There was a limitless knowing and presence. . .

Apparently I was found satisfactory. . .which made me very happy that I hadn't in some way embarrassed or disappointed Maharaji. . .I was clearly a student of some sort given over to Maharaji's care and the elder had come to check on my progress.

We left and that was the end of it. Maharaji didn't speak of it and we went on about our day's business. I had the feeling that I would not have been able to find that place again if I tried. . .The place might not truly exist on the physical plane and the whole thing might be an apparition created at the time so that I wouldn't freak. . .(?) don't know, probably never will. The fact is that I never did anything of my own volition during this time of living with Maharaji in the gunny sack.

There was no particular ending to the vision. . .but then it wasn't there anymore. I tried a few times to get back into the vision, but wasn't able to. Perhaps simply a meal to be eaten and then go on without saving the dishes, napkins, menus. Thank you God for most this amazing day.

12/15/90 – Saturday – Day 21

Course – 305 degrees west. Latitude – 13 degrees, 09 minutes north. Longitude 49 degrees west. 585 miles to go.

After yesterday's excitement, the wind has calmed down. Still doing over five knots, but it's slower. Will take longer to St. Lucia. . .Lo Mano de Dios.

At 20:00 hours. . .sails down, the motor back on. God I love being here although I am more than tired of them. . .Oh my love, let's go sailing!

12/16/90—Sunday – Day 22

We have two and a half to three days to go. Now 18:00 hours and we've motored about 38 hours. Feels like we're just grinding it out. We've got Monday and Tuesday and then we'll probably get there by noon on Wednesday. If the wind picks up, we could be a few hours earlier. If need be, I think we'll motor all the way rather than go slower.

Who knows, it all depends on the moods of a 46-year-old drunken BIG BOY. Boy, do I have a bunch of questions for Emmanuel and Maharaji!

The romantic in me wants to surprise you at Judith's. We'll see what happens. If I can't make it to the party (plane ticket), I'll call you at the party.

12/17/90 – Monday – Day 23

301 miles to go. This thing has been an interesting ordeal and passage. . .more than simply a pleasure cruise. Island hopping is for pleasure. . .this is a whole different number.

I was just figuring out how to surprise you at 89th Street and I was imagining us hugging and I started to cry.

12/18/90—Tuesday – Day 24

We've sailed 2,585 miles from Gran Canaria.

So finally, we're motor sailing the last 40 hours or so, and last night at about 1 a.m., we ran out of fuel. They didn't know how much fuel was left! Marx Brothers again!

We're moving along. . .I'm going to be able to make the party maybe. . .then we run out of fuel within the last 24 hours. . .I look up and sort of smile, shrug and say to Maharaji, "Okay, another let-go level. Okay, okay, okay, okay. You win."

Apparently there is a reserve of diesel in the hollow keel. . .BUT, they don't know how much. So, after deciding to sail (at about four knots) until 18:00 hours and then put on the engine which has 100 miles worth of fuel (maybe) within five minutes, the sails are coming down and the motor is on full power.

I ask Bill if we'd use less diesel if we didn't go so fast? He becomes very angry and tells me not to panic. . .I tell him slowly and clearly that asking a question is not panicking. . .and then I realize that he is panicked by the uncertainty of the situation and must appear decisive lest anyone sense that he doesn't know what he's doing. . .therefore, do something powerful and decisive – ENGINE FULL SPEED AHEAD!

By everyone's reckoning we have 150 miles to go and about 100 miles worth of fuel which we are now burning. At 75 miles I will point out we have only 25 left. . .I certainly don't want to run out with 25 miles to go. . .We will need some fuel to motor into the marina and dock this thing.

This whole thing has been emergency to emergency. . .what a drag.

I haven't mentioned how embarrassed I am that I have done this to myself. I almost walked off the boat 12 hours before the start back in Canaria, but figured I couldn't get another ride or get my $200 in food money back.

Interesting, for maybe the first time in my life, I don't give a shit whatever they think, feel, do or say. . .and I include all those spiritual levels where we are all one, not seeing any differences. I feel no obligation towards them. Some day I might pray for them, but I don't think I will make any more effort to relieve their suffering. . .I feel willing to just leave them to their mess.

Let them go their way and I will go mine. If the Gods create some reason for me to have more business with them, so be it. But if left to me, I wouldn't cross the street to say hello. I also wouldn't cross the street to avoid them either. I simply feel "I have no further interest in you or business with you."

Very freeing. I've never really allowed myself that freedom – the freedom to see someone else in pain and not feel compelled to try to fix it. There is a Jewish requirement that one has a responsibility to "heal the world." I think it's – "tikun olam." It is a commandment. It falls right in with my personal historical drive to make everyone in my family happy, and, of course no one was or is.

The thread of that requirement has permeated everything so that I have always felt an additional obligation to go the extra mile to try to make everything work out for everyone.

On one level, the Infinite Compassion of the Buddha is wonderful, and I have that too, and there is a part of me that was compelled to do something. I couldn't just let someone suffer and say, "That's how it is" and leave it there. I'd always carry a part of the suffering if I couldn't do anything to fix it.

Fortunately the wind picked up and we were able to sail the last 50 miles, without the motor, into Rodney Bay Harbor on St. Lucia, where the ARC rally finished. At the entrance to the harbor, Bill and Ed broke out the brandy bottles and were congratulating themselves for their successful voyage.

I pointed that that we had one last dangerous maneuver to accomplish, that we had to set up lines and fenders to dock the boat in a crowded harbor of wood and fiber glass vessels. They forgot that our boat was made of heavy steel and could crush them.

Grudgingly, they agreed with me and we set up the dock lines and fenders. Once more I was just a pain in the ass to them, and once more I saved them from serious harm. Then I took the helm to steer us in the last 50 feet as we almost smashed into boats tied up on either side of us.

When we finally tied up, we were welcomed as heroes by the rally committee, like all the other rally boats which completed the 2,700 mile voyage. But I knew we were really a comic book ship of fools. I was done. It was another overtime day for my guardian angel.

The moment that the boat is safely and securely tied to the dock, I find myself sitting down near the bow and just sobbing in relief and appreciation that my journey with them is over and I no longer am vulnerable to their drunkenness.

I have been able to get checked through Customs and am cleared to leave the boat and be on my way. It is 10:30 p.m. and I am packed and gone from the boat within 15 minutes. I have a place to stay nearby and will look into flights in the morning. . .later I find out that I may be able to get a flight at 7 a.m. to Puerto Rico and from there a flight to NYC. . .which comes to pass. I make the party in NYC on time, surprising you and myself. . .thank you God for most these amazing days!

V. Sailing Stories

Twenty Years Sailing with Bill Wraith IV

When he was 58 and working as a boat captain out of Tortola in the British Virgin Islands, Michael Projansky went to work as captain of a yacht in 1997 for a wealthy financial executive named Bill Wraith IV. He was the American President of Nomura in the United States, a big Japanese financial company with its US headquarters at the World Financial Center in Lower Manhattan.

Wraith was learning how to sail away from his high pressure job, and was looking for a boat captain to manage and help him sail his yacht named "Chaos," a 38-foot sloop built in Sweden.

When Bill's previous boat captain Dan Harper introduced him to Michael Projansky, Waith had "an intuition that he was the right boat captain for me. Michael was 18 years older, mature and well educated. I felt that I could trust him. He turned out to be one of the very best friends of my entire life."

Over the next 20 years, they spent a lot of time together on Wraith's yacht, sailing the entire coast of the Northeast from New Jersey to Nova Scotia, and from Nantucket, where Wraith had a cottage and spent parts of 20 summers, to the Caribbean, where they sometimes sailed in Michael's own boat. Wraith recalls that Michael was very strong and in good health, until he started to get tired more easily in about 2013 and became disabled in 2017. Before that sudden decline, Wraith says, "Michael was stronger than I was, even though I was 18 years younger. When we took ten-mile hikes in Maine, between sailing trips, I always had trouble keeping up with him."

"We spent a lot of time sailing together, just the two of us. I heard all his stories, his spiritual adventures in India, his work with Ram Dass in Colorado, his visions. Wraith kept his confidence, and Michael always protected Bill's privacy, a discreet behavior Wraith much appreciated.

Wraith recalled two "epic sails" with Michael – one heart-stopping trip 90 miles up the St. John River from the "reversing falls" at its mouth at the Bay of Fundy, where the tide rises and falls 24 feet every day over a stone ledge; and another unforgettable 300-mile open sea sail from Jonesport, Maine, to Lockport, Nova Scotia, during which a whale and a large school of dolphins swam peacefully along side their boat.

Bill Wraith IV, owner of yacht "Chaos" in background on Maine Coast

But when Michael's health started to deteriorate in 2013-2015, Wraith recalls, "It was deeply troubling to me. But we kept sailing as long as Michael could be safe on a boat at sea, and I did more and more of the work. I got so connected to Michael that I wanted to take care of him and kept paying his salary. He had no pension plan and never asked for anything. Michael would call a mock executive committee meeting once a year, and we would agree to work together for another year, with a handshake."

Like Michael's many friends, Bill Wraith had a special fondness for him. "He is one of the few 100% adults I have met in my life. He is a very thoughtful man, with his unique bearing, a very moral and ethical man. He did an excellent job for me and for my boat. And he was a kind of father figure for me too."

Editor's Note: *From a telephone interview of Bill Wraith IV by Jim Ottaway, Jr. on July 26, 2019*

Bill Giles and Murder

I'm on the helm, at the wheel of a 55-foot steel sail boat. A few thousand miles from anywhere, alone in the cockpit at night, drinking a cup of coffee, enjoying the quiet. Bill comes up from below, puts his coffee down. It is clear that he wants to speak to me. Bill, at six foot six, a 285-pound ex-rugby player going to fat from muscle. He tells me a story about when he was a merchant mariner on ships on the ocean; usually 15 men at once on these big boats. Every now and then, they would agree that they would not like somebody and would play a game they called "shunning" where they wouldn't talk to this person or act like he was there. They wouldn't listen to him so they would avoid him. This would go on a week or so and then one morning at breakfast, someone would ask "I haven't seen Joe, what happened with him?" Then one of the other men would say, "I don't know, he must have gotten lost" and the others would say, "Fuck him, never liked him."

What this meant was that he had been thrown overboard. This is a game they played. Bill was telling me this story, I think to point out to me that he was willing to push me overboard too. It seemed clear that he had done it at least once and the reason that he might push me over is that I knew that he didn't know what he was doing, that he was faking it, even though he was the owner and nominal captain of the boat.

It then became very interesting for me because I spent the next week or so having to decide whether to carry a weapon. Of course I would fight back, I would resist him. Am I prepared to kill him if he tries to kill me? Then I recognized that no, I wouldn't carry a weapon and if he threw me overboard, so be it.

Now what do I believe? Do I just die or does a school of dolphins save me, or an airliner crash land next to me? Well, that never came to pass. Who knows?

If There is Anger, There is Fear

So, I am on this sailboat with a bunch of drunken Englishmen. I can't stand them and they can't stand me. I spend as much time as I can all the way forward, holding onto the head sail, bouncing up and down as the boat goes through the waves. Occasionally I feel ecstatic. It is glorious. Beyond glorious. It is a magical space and I know that I'm of God and that I am not here. I am there, I am here, I am there simultaneously.

The energy was magical and I thought of the other guys on the boat who I really had trouble with. I realized that they were just little boys who didn't know what they were doing. I felt so benign and so loving toward them. I realized that my job was to help them get through, however I could. I was struck by it. And then I suddenly found that state of mind changed. I went back to being justified in my anger at them. They were drunks. They were pigs. They were just dreadful!

And I thought about myself being so vulnerable to the conditions of life. I thought about it and thought about it and thought about it. And I said, "Hmm, that is interesting. I notice that when I am loving, when I am feeling ecstatic, I'm not afraid of anything. There is no fear. But when I am angry at them, I am furious because I think that they are dangerous." And I realized that there is only anger when there is fear. If there is anger, there is fear. Look for the fear, do not justify the anger.

It was like being in the Tibetan Wheel of Life, going from the heavenly realm to the hell realm in one swell swoop all depending on my attitude. I realized that the issue is not outside myself. It is always within me. When I am not fearful, there is no danger. When I think there is danger and I am fearful, the apparently smart thing is to identify and distance myself from the danger.

Bermuda Northeaster

We had had a picture perfect eight days from Tortola to Bermuda where we stopped for provisions, fuel, a rest and weather reports.

The weather warned of a northeaster, which meant wind against the Gulf Stream which is a powerful river within the ocean. Jim, the skipper, had activated a phone call with his girlfriend and insisted that we needed to leave immediately. I warned him about the weather, but he said we will be all right. He lied.

Within a day, we had both the weather and the Gulf Stream against us. Approximately five knots of Gulf Stream which stood the waves up as high as I had ever seen.

We sailed up the back of each wave to the top, turned hard right to starboard for five seconds and then sailed down the front of the wave. Up, down, up down, up down – it was exhausting. When Jim, the skipper, relieved me after an hour, I laid down on my bunk knowing that I would not sleep. I could at least rest a bit.

I could feel every shudder and creak of the boat, and I wrote an imaginary letter to the president of the boat making company thanking him for putting an extra layer of fiberglass on the hull. The Catalina we were sailing was not built for ocean sailing, but it was holding up.

We obviously got home.

Michael on yacht in Caribbean

Years later, when rummaging through some equipment, I came across a reminder of this trip, and called Frank Butler, President of Catalina Yachts, in California. Using my doctor's title, I got through the secretaries and spoke to him. After asking him if he had a few minutes, I related this story and thanked him for building a better boat than people thought. He was glad that I made his day since he was talking that day to accountants who were trying to downgrade the boat by lowering the standards.

Ocean Storm

It is hard to tell this story without clichés but holding the wheel more tightly than normal, I realized we were already in it – we were not going to be in it – but we were in it. The wind had picked up to the 30s and 40s and may go higher; 45 miles an hour of wind speed is the limit at which we can steer the boat. Beyond that, it is a matter of trusting the structure of the vessel. At that point, we need to restructure the sails, reduce their size, lock the wheel and go below and let the boat be thrashed by wind and waves. We went below.

A wave hits the bow and throws us 20 degrees off and then the stern gets hit and spins back again.

There is no rhyme nor reason and no predictability. There is always the threat of death. The ideas that pervade about safety gear are simply obstacles when the weather gets heavy. We entered a realm where other forces take over. It is similar to the dead zone in mountain climbing when you climb too high without oxygen.

What compels us, and other people, to come out here? Bad weather is inevitable yet we push the edges constantly, not the edges of our own courage or bravery or challenges like that, but the edges of experience. It is an exploration deep within ourselves to meet parts of ourselves lying there dormant. I have been amazed that I don't freak out, I get scared but I don't freak out. I did not know that about myself. Yet there is no assurance that I won't freak out or die in the next heavy storm.

VI. Other Experiences

Author's Note: *This book is not a collection of **all** the unusual experiences I have had. It is instead about special states of perception that I have been given during my life. I have been lucky to have the following vivid experiences.*

Paul

I used the glass door of the memorial chapel as a mirror to make sure I was presentable. The hair was a little long, but it was okay. A lot of times in my life I've looked a whole lot worse. I passed a satisfactory balance of clean and respectable and slightly avant garde. I had read the Style Times and made my choices. I was shy about going in, but just pushed ahead.

This was a funeral for a graduate professor, Dr. Paul Frisch, who had been a powerful force in a lot of lives so I knew there would be many others there who I had not seen since getting my degree. He was an exciting and charismatic teacher of psychology. I expected to see many other previous students, and along with that came a lot of self consciousness, wondering and not a little trepidation.

The self consciousness came easy since I was about to walk into a room filled with a bunch of clinical psychologists who were no more sure than I about what to do, feel or say, but made lots of judgments. As I pushed the door open, I felt the familiar need to find a bathroom, having nothing to do with my bladder. I was nervous and wanted to put this off for another minute.

I'd been to very few funerals. Death was not a place I visited very much. Being in my mid-30s, I was much more involved with notions about life rather than death. Death was something for other people. In my life, death was very theoretical, as were most things. Nice and theoretical.

But self consciousness, that was not theoretical. That was up front and center. My breathing was shallow and high in my chest. My shoulders were up a bit and my feet didn't really feel solid on the ground. My face was a bit flushed and I could feel the heat. Still in the foyer, I looked around and saw the chapel off to the left, with rows of padded folded chairs, flowers, and the plain coffin at the front of the room. Straight ahead was an open double door into the reception room with small groups standing around. I went into the bathroom off to my right.

I splashed some cold water on my face. Looking in the mirror, I realized that we were all in the evaluating and judging business and that we got into it often because we were always evaluating and judging ourselves and wanted to get some leverage on the whole business.

As psychologists, we were the official clear-eyed objective helpers. Paul knew better. He knew that we were all just trying to hack our way through the underbrush of our own lives and that if we could relax a little about that fact, we wouldn't be as much of a danger to ourselves and others. If we could stop judging ourselves so harshly, we could perhaps actually become of some use to others.

This was not an easy communication in a discipline trying to sell itself and the culture on the idea that a science of the mind was possible and that was what we were all about. Paul knew that the art of opening the heart/mind was more the point, and that science of mind as practiced in the West was a self deluded marketing strategy.

Breathing closer to normal, I entered the reception room with the same self consciousness, but now I was simply into it rather than feeling the discomfort of anticipation. This was all very familiar to me. I was afraid of being judged, found wanting and somehow being humiliated by someone or something in the situation. I looked around and moved towards a group of familiar faces. Some initial sense of sanctuary.

Greetings, how have you been, it must be six years since we saw each other. . .and then a silence, coming out of the shock we all were feeling. Paul was a vibrant man in his 50s when a heart attack came and his life stopped.

He had been an intimate young father figure to all of us, and we weren't supposed to be here at this funeral. More likely a publishing party for a creative cutting edge book about an esoteric psychological issue, or an opening night party for a play he might have written. This wasn't supposed to happen until later, when we were older, more settled, safer. Too soon. But here we were. Paul was dead.

Many of us had been in therapy with him. The mish mosh of feelings last a very long time if the therapy is good, and Paul was good. He gave you a run for your money. Challenging, teasing, engaging, fostering an intimacy of thought and feeling. One felt as though this guy really was interested and was right here with you, struggling through the scary parts with you. A relentlessly honest mirror to reflect back the distortions and self securing stories we all tell ourselves. . .but all done with the sad smile of one who wrestled with his own stuff.

After a while, I approached the couch where his wife was sitting, receiving condolences. We didn't know each other well, so there didn't seem to be much to share. Not being comfortable enough in myself, I said some appropriate words, she nodded and I got up for someone else to sit. Now I wonder what it must have been like for her sitting there receiving everyone's attempts to express too much in a few sentences while she was going through whatever her pains and confusions were. Oh my goodness, how little I knew about anything and how hard I felt I had to jump ahead with my mind and try to know what I had not yet experienced. Whew.

Not wanting to stand around with others and feeling somewhat like a spectator watching something they shouldn't be seeing, i.e., a wife mourning, I left the room and went into the sanctuary. My own connection with Paul had been very individual and I wanted to feel whatever I had with him without being susceptible to someone else's movie. I wanted my own distortions and projections, not someone else's.

The room was empty and I could "talk" with him alone. At that time, I had been doing a lot of meditation and yoga and was comfortable sitting cross-legged with eyes closed and simply observing whatever transpired. I took a few deep breaths and wiped my hands over my hair three times which helped me to get quiet and attentive.

Very quickly I found myself in a large open cave-like space in a very high mountain. It was very remote and one could only get there by being brought. It was ancient and felt sacred. There was a processional of elders, human angels who had been taking birth at various intervals and doing loving work with humans since the beginning. They would leave for a time and then return to this endless processional.

There was no drama, no hurry, no anxiety, the calm simple working out of human holiness. These were beings who had finally achieved the ability to live on Earth with love, compassion, integrity and peace, the way we all yearn for. There is a poster of a beautiful Che Guevara with a caption saying, "The responsibility of every revolutionary is to live their life as though the revolution has already been won." These were beings who had vanquished the forces within themselves that had kept them from holiness. They were free, so they could surrender to and serve the deepest needs of others.

Dressed in simple robes, they were nominally men and women, but most were past that distinction. This was a sacred space and I felt great respect and gratitude within me to be able to be there. I was not part of it. I was being allowed to see. I saw Paul enter the cave and move forward toward the processional which kept moving slowly onward. He was received as a respected younger, but full member of the group. A space opened up and he re-entered the flow. He had done his work and was received back home. He would continue in the endless processional until it was time for him to come to Earth again.

After a while, I slowly opened my eyes and all the self consciousness was gone. I missed him. I loved him and I was glad we had walked together here on Earth for as long as we did. I had been afraid of him and what I was afraid he would show me before I felt ready.

His message to me, both then and now, was that of course I was safe simply because I was who I was. I was full and good and I could be more generous in giving both myself and others permission to simply be who we are. I bowed my head and thanked him for all of it. I went back into the room and greeted the others, this time, without fear, really glad to see them.

Later, I shared my experience with a few people and some heard me with open ears and others not. I knew what I had seen was true and it was okay if some of the others would rather not see my movie. Something could be absolutely true for me and be irrelevant foolishness for someone else.

There had always been a need in me that we all find out the truth of something and agree on it. I had struggled with that many times in my youth. Many of my truths didn't seem so popular or interesting, but too challenging. The resulting self doubt would often lead to harder feelings than were ever intended. My experience with Paul in the sanctuary helped me soften some of that old pattern.

Years later, I met Paul's wife accidentally in a gift shop. I related the story about what had happened for me at the funeral. The look on her face conveyed a concern that I had gone wandering too much somewhere along the road. She had very little interest in me or my narrative.

By this time, I could hear and see it and know it had little to do with me. As my three-year-old grandson will occasionally say when he sees someone sad or left out, "It's okay. . .It's okay."

I wonder where my grandson was in the processional that day so many years ago.

Meditation in New Paltz

I had been meditating off and on in formal and informal situations for 40 odd years when I found myself in New Paltz with a rag tag group of mainly inexperienced people, and my judging mind was disappointed. I went anyway and found a cornucopia of special people.

I feel in love with Manuela, who died fairly soon. With others in the group, I found myself opening my heart to them, and I realized that my guardian angel had brought me to the right place. There are men and women in the group who do not have an esoteric grounding, but there was something important about them. For half an hour, they sit each day.

Old friendships deepened and transformed, and new friendships were slow going at first but we warmed up to each other.

I came to see that my meditation is now more focused on opening my heart rather then following any creed. And the title of a book by Ram Dass came to mind – "The Only Dance There Is."

I had been obsessed with particulars such as the curve of my arms and hands, holding the right posture and modulation of my breath and quieting my mind. In this new situation, I started to see that the more essential question was simply being present; sitting together in a group is a commitment of each one for all and all for one. Romantic to think of us as D'Artagnan and his buddies!

I was struck by people taking time out of their semi-busy schedules to be there at the early morning meditation.

It was interesting when I could no longer walk into the room, I sat in my car outside during the mediation to be there at the beginning and at the end. I developed a different loyalty toward the practice.

A deepening appreciation developed. Simply being present was in itself an act of faith. I bow my head.

With New Paltz Meditation group of friends.
From left, Jim O'Dowd, Mary Cotton Miller, Michael.

A Molecule of Shit

This is a story from many years ago, but it is true right now. And strangely, it is sort of definitive of what I am going through. I feel so bound by my physical process that I cannot really travel, move, or do anything which is familiar. It's a very disconcerting feeling. I am immobilized even though I have an electric wheelchair and go to meals. I cannot leave the building.

So, 40 years ago, I was living with my kids in New Paltz, NY and I was returning from lower Manhattan.

I realized that I would be passing by Judith Stanton's place on 89th Street on the way uptown to the George Washington Bridge. She was somewhat of an elder and traveler with me in spiritual concerns. I decided to stop over and say hello. We greeted each other at the door and she immediately asked, "Do you want to take ketamine?"

"Sure" I said; whatever that meant. I didn't know what ketamine was but I trusted her completely. She said "okay" and brought me inside. "Take your pants halfway down," she told me. She suddenly shot me in the ass with a fluid and said, "Lie down real quick, you will need to, because it comes on very fast. I'll be in the other room taking the same stuff and you can call if you need me but you will soon see that there is not much I can do."

It was like being on an acid trip, but on speed. Everything was in fast forward, racing from one mind state to another to another to another. And each mind state did not change until I said "yes" to each one of them.

At one point I found myself as a molecule of shit, part of a clump of dirt, stuck inside the hoof of a burro. The molecule next to me was absolutely close to me. There was no spaciousness, no mobility, and no sense of choice. I was just stuck in what I was stuck in, maybe forever, I didn't know.

At first I recoiled from the constriction of it until I finally softened and opened to it. I said, "Okay. If that is what it is, that's what it is." And once I said this, my mind state changed into something else. And now I am feeling that same sense of, "I am where I am, where I am, where I am and it will or it won't change." And even if it does change, it won't.

Reminiscing with Ananda

At one point after we had been divorced for some years, I found myself feeling resentful toward Ananda because I wanted to have an experience with her that I thought I could no longer have. I always looked forward to having shared years together so that we could look back – proverbially – sitting on the front porch and talking over what we had shared. However the circumstances did not allow for that since our living experiences were now separate.

But lo and behold, she came back to New Paltz to live out the end of her life and in fact, affection seemed to be legal tender between us. No referral crap – just affection. I once again became her best friend.

Michael with Ananda, his first wife, two years before she died in 2017

With all the activity at our daughter Amara's house where Ananda was living, it was clear it would fall to me to often feed

Ananda, and we would go to the Plaza Diner to order dinner and sit there an like an old couple and review old stories. So what I had dreamed about came to pass!

Those were very tender times.

Family

Watching Amara with Asher, when he was first born – about 14 years ago in their very simple house in Woodstock.

Amara was bending over Asher and calling him "lovey lovely." I watched from across the room and saw that they were bathed in light. At that moment, a deep voice inside me said, "That's it. That is what I didn't get in my life." The same deep voice came from within and said, "You are getting it now," and I began to understand how enriching fatherhood can be. It was a first and very vivid sense of ongoing family.

My White Jaguar

One summer day in 1975 when I was living in an apartment building on Huguenot Street in New Paltz, I saw a beautiful white Jaguar four-door sedan driving by. I ran out on the street, stopped the driver and told him I wanted a Jaguar like his car some day.

The very distinguished, well-dressed man told me it was a 1950 Mark V Saloon model, and said, "Maybe some day." I noticed that his companion in the passenger seat was a very beautiful woman.

Fast forward ten years later. I always read the Classic Cars for Sale classified ads in the New York Times Sports Section, and notice one day a 1950 Jaguar sedan for sale for $15,000.

So I call the owner/seller in Virginia and tell him that I once saw a white Jaguar sedan just like the car in the New York Times ad driving down my street in New Paltz, and that I dreamed of buying one some day.

I told the owner/seller that a very distinguished man and beautiful woman were driving their Jaguar ten years earlier in New Paltz. "That was my father and mother! My father just died," he shouted over the phone.

When I told him I would love to buy his father's car, but couldn't possibly afford $15,000, he said, "What can you pay me for it?" After some fast calculation I answered, "Maybe $4,500."

"Come and get it," he answered. "I want you to have it." And so I drove that magnificent white Jaguar around New Paltz for a few years. Truck drivers and strangers on the street would give me a thumbs up as I drove by.

When it got too expensive to keep up, I sold it for $7,500.

Michael driving his white Jaguar sedan, about 1985.

Emmanuel – Different Task

Pat and Emmanuel and I had recently done a series of workshops in which Emmanuel had asked me to answer the questions that people posed. Although I didn't channel Emmanuel, I did receive knowledge from elsewhere and shared this with people. I started to think that Emmanuel was going to train me to be a channel. He said, "Human beings are still more comfortable with keeping humanity and divinity separate but will occasionally accept a voice from on high disseminating wisdom. My dear channel Pat and I made such an agreement where Pat has become the human receptacle of what appears to be divine wisdom. You Michael, have come for a different purpose. You are here to join humanity and divinity in one person. That is your work."

When God told Jonah to go speak in God's name, Jonah ran away and was swallowed up by the giant whale. I have been running away for 30 years. Having grown up with the usual belief that divinity was a steady state, that you do not go in and out of it, but that you are either in it or you are not. I had too much impurity. In the ensuing years, I have come to see that we do divine things sometimes and when we do, we are divinity. It is just that we do not stay there in a steady state. We go in and out of it. In that way, I am finally taking on the mantle that Emmanuel gave me 30 years ago.

This is true for some other people. Not just me.

Portraits

We are standing on the stair landing with a soft northern light splashing down on his face. I have a camera in hand and I'm trying to have him open his face a little more to me. "Please look up at me." He is afraid and can only tilt his head to the side, as though he would enter into some space in his shoulder from which he could look out at me from a safer place.

Looking at the light falling on him, I see his beauty and wonder how to have his soft smile pour out for me and the camera. The light, filtered through the trees outside, has a soft pensive quality that is perfect for what I am trying to achieve. The only problem is that he is afraid and is somewhat like a deer in the headlights.

I am a psychologist consultant to the Head Start program created for the migrant workers of Eastern Long Island. The school is in an old Victorian house in Southampton that is quite grand in style, but has fallen on hard times. Christmas is coming and I had decided to do soft portraits of the kids and give them as presents. I was hoping to give each mother a framed "art" portrait of her child, but it sure wasn't working so far.

Knowing not to push, I took a rubber ball out of my pocket and began bouncing it. I bounced if off my head, the wall, the stairs behind him. He watched, clearly wanting it, but having no idea how to approach me for it. I was an adult and adults hit kids. He had probably been hit more in his first three years than I had been in my whole life.

No, approaching a strange adult white man for something he wanted was not in his frame of reference. Without meaning to, many of these overworked, poor mothers taught their kids how hard a hand could be. Many of them simply watched out carefully, as he was doing with me now.

The ball got stuck on a stair up behind him. I reach for it but it is obvious I would never be able to get it. He watches carefully as I burlesque my attempts to move to get it. After a few "attempts" I raise my head towards the ball and ask him with my hands and eyes if he would get it. He pulls back, looks at the ball, at me, and then goes to get the ball. When he returns, he stands in front of me shyly, sweetly, but far enough away that he can duck if my hands are as treacherous as others have been.

I reach for the ball, but again, I show that I can't reach it. I try again and again, but clearly my arms won't reach the ball or him. I start to make funny reaching noises and little whimpering sounds when I fail again and again. He begins to move forward and back in a tentative teasing.

We start to laugh at each other and enjoy the game we have created and I see the beauty I was looking for before. There it is. I picked up my camera and gestured to him a question of "Is it okay to take a picture?"

He gets serious again, so I mock grab the ball again while framing him in the viewfinder. The soft smile comes back. He has control over me and the ball. I'm not a hitter and for this moment it's okay. And the camera clicks and we both smile.

As I lower the camera, I realize I am looking up at his face and there is no longer a little boy there. There is an African prince looking down on one of his subjects about whom he is pleased. The difference in the height of our eyes, mine now just a few inches below his allows him to come to his full height. Before, I was viewing him from slightly above and it made all the difference. He then had to be a little boy to my man. My goodness, the power of position in personal relationships.

I remembered to stay slightly below the kids and had them choose whatever toys or clothes we had, and to let them stand or sit wherever and however they wanted. My reward was a cascade of portraits of royalty, Dahomey queens, Yoruba princes, kings, queens, and a few court jesters thrown in.

I might otherwise have gotten "nice" pictures of some poor black kids. The mothers were as pleased with the portraits as I was.

Terry

We are walking, two 12-year-olds in 1951, probably the first time alone together in our lives although we had been in the same class since kindergarten. Both smart, decent athletes, presentable, middle class, white, we would both be expected to go on and be successful in the post-war Westchester world in which we were growing up.

Both in the uniform of the time, high-top sneakers, what used to be called basketball shoes, dungarees with cuffs carefully folded up twice, tee shirts, hair short and parted, not crewcuts, carrying our baseball gloves, with hats, mine Dodger, his Yankee, on our heads. Coming from a game we had just played, the conversation was about the game, hits, players, outs, the usual post-game banter.

At first the conversation was neutral and then a contention began between us. There was always some tension between us. We "got along" but there was no affection. We had always been competitors in class, probably more clearly for me since I was the more erratic in school work, he always being among the first two or three to "get them all right" and I often being there, but not always. I was the better natural athlete, better balance, less formal, more responsive to whatever the moment called for. Like most boys we had "sized each other up" over the years, weighing our chances with each other in case we had to fight.

Both being the youngest of three, with strong, bright, competitive siblings, he with two sisters, I with two brothers, we always felt the pressure of striving to catch up, measure up, to be taken seriously.

The contention became an argument and we began shoving each other in the chest and then we were on the ground wrestling, pulling, pushing, trying to get on top. We were a match for each other in strength, neither of us being officially strong kids. At first, there was almost a desultory, just messing around quality to it. We weren't serious. Neither of us wanting to really hurt the other. Then he got me in a hammerlock around the neck and head. As he squeezed to establish his hold, anger at the pain and coming humiliation of being beaten took hold and I pushed my fist into his neck as hard as I could. As I kept pushing, I put everything into it since, at the moment, it was all I had. . ."and he shouldn't have started it anyway. . ."

He released enough so I could twist myself out of the grip and we ended up rolling around on the strip of grass between the sidewalk and the busy street, probably only five feet from the traffic going by.

After some time of our grappling with each other, I ended up on top of him in an "official" winning position. I was sitting on his stomach and was starting to pin his arms down with his hands by his head. He was bucking underneath me as hard as he could. Like a rider on a bull, I had learned his rhythm and adjusted and held my position. I had the leverage necessary to pin his wrists so that he was powerless.

I looked in his eyes and realized that I hated him. I was beating him and I was glad. I was "getting even." He had won so many times in class, had received whatever prizes of the moment so often with an air of entitlement, that I had hated, envied him. He had so often looked over at me with an air of superiority, saying, "See, I won again. I always win more than you. Yeah, you're smart too and talented in some off the wall ways, but where it counts, I'm better and I'm going to win the prizes. I'll be up, and you'll be down."

I held him down and established that I had him. I had beaten him. He was under me and couldn't get up no matter how hard he struggled. And then I pushed down on him, into him. I wanted to imprint into him that he had lost to me and that I had won. It was like branding a steer, but I didn't just want to burn the outer hide, I wanted to burn it into him.

"There, how do you like that? Take it in. Hurt. Feel yourself down off your high horse, where you're no big deal, not special. Feel inferiority. Feel the knowing that you're missing something necessary for the times that will come, even if you don't know what they are, that you already know that it probably won't work out comfortably for you. That there will be a lot of pain and confusion. There, you sonofabitch. Feel what it feels like. There."

In the play, "The Boys Next Door," there is a scene where one of the characters, a borderline functioning man living in a protected residence is being hurried to finish something and join the group. As he is being badgered, he runs himself around the stage into confusion and finally stops the frenetic movement and says very softly with a cry, ". . .It be hard. . .and I not ready. . ."

Decorum required that I let him up as soon as I had pinned him after getting an acknowledgement that I had "won." As I held him, I looked again into his eyes and saw fear. I saw that he had not ever been in this place and he was scared. He saw that I hated him and could really hurt him.

He saw that life was a messier place than the words on a page, or numbers in a column and he was sentenced to live within it. He started to panic. I had really scared him. I was implacable and I had bested him and I hated him and there was no guarantee that I was going to let him up or that I wouldn't keep pushing into him to cause him more pain.

I saw the panic and let him up.

I don't know what happened immediately after, but we never talked again. I hid the experience away somewhere until it came back many years later when I got the notice for a high school reunion and saw his name. . .and with it surfaced the shame I had hidden away in favor of victory at the age of 12.

Walla Walla Wheat Fields

In the summer of 1956, after my junior year in high school, my brother Arnold called and asked me what I was doing. I had been caddying at a local golf club. He suggested I get on an airplane and fly to Washington State where he was with a college dorm mate working on the ranches. "I can get you work and it will be interesting," he said.

What an entirely different world that section of southeastern Washington was, filled with wheat ranches, and it was reaping time. I became part of a crew working for a man named Gerald Gibson. When his parents died, he had given up his medical practice in Seattle to go home to Walla Walla and work the ranch. He had two rules – no racing and don't shop in town to get anything (he would get it for us. I and we were expected to honor the rules. He had a bunk house for us all and breakfast was wonderful. He brought good lunches out to us in the fields and then we had healthy dinners back at the bunkhouse. I worked hard that summer standing up on a combine dragged by a tractor.

One time, I bought cigarettes in town and when I came out to get back in the truck, it was gone and I called the police to report a stolen truck. He had stolen the truck and told the police. I went to the police station and was kept there until he came for me after six or seven hours, at about 8:00 pm that night. Being a high school kid from Westchester County, New York, I did not realize it was a failing of mine not to honor my word. An interesting anecdote in my summer.

A week later, my brother and I decided to race back to the bunk house. The next morning at breakfast, Mr. Gibson told me to pack our things and he took us back to town. "You are good workers, but I cannot trust you. Like any other renegade, I have to cut you lose from the group." He left us there. A good lesson in integrity! He was a good teacher.

At another time that same summer, we were driving from Walla Walla down the Pacific Coast in our slightly modified MG that Arnold and I had bought back in New York. I drove down Route 1 as fast as I could since there was a truck behind me beeping. Telling me that I was driving too slow. He kept up with us and kept beeping. I finally pulled over and let him pass along with four other truckers. I realized he was a master driver and I had held them up; he was not the only one I was holding back. I recognized that

they were master drivers and there were masters in lots of fields –
including these truck drivers – spread around the world. It took a
while for the arrogance of youth to wear away.

Author's Note: *We are surrounded by masters, silently doing what*
they know how to do well. July 2, 1019.

Too Serious for Mind Games

It becomes a funny situation when you are caught. The only thing
you have is the stuff in your mind. You have nothing else. Nothing
else is happening. It seems like the only thing to do is to play it out
and yet, at the same time, there is an inherent hesitation about
playing it all out. Everything has been so temporary. The idea
about being stuck inside a space that is both claustrophobic and
too spacious at once; it is an interesting human dilemma.

There is no way of raising it to a higher level of abstraction.
There is no way of getting around it. Cannot go forward, cannot go
back. It is too real, too compelling. It is the end of life. Yet, it is too
spacious and there isn't the safety net of thinking, "Well, you will
wake up and you will be sober." Once again, just "brown is brown."
It is what it is.

Interesting place.

I remember Pat (my second wife) and I once went to the Grand
Canyon and it just blew our minds. It was just too big. We couldn't
get our heads around it.

Out on the ocean, during a storm, you occasionally get a little bit
of that sense too. Just too big, just too big. There is no conceptual
notion that can capture it all. Too serious for mind games. Thus,
the beginning of a new vocabulary.

There are issues that go beyond our minds. They are heart matters. There occasionally are situations or circumstances that must be dealt with and cannot be up-leveled by some mind trick. These are heart matters. Two nouns. The heart must be activated, the seat of true wisdom that resides in all of us.

Heart Matters

If you are attending to something really serious then it is a question of the heart. It is a question of a wisdom that is much beyond the mind. Mind is just filled with confusing and contradictory images. Just thoughts to play with and not to be taken too seriously. As we know, there is a wisdom inside of us that knows that our mind is not the seat of real power even though we act as if it were. We come to a place where heart is more important than mind. It is a heart matter.

Rush Hour

Darting, pushing, shoving, no one acknowledges anyone else. Everyone moves purposely forward, head down, bent over slightly, jostling. Bodies lightly bouncing off each other's space.

Everyone in a rush going as fast as they can but very controlled, don't want to invade or be invaded. Have to get to work, no time to get caught in anything, become part of a story on the 6 o'clock news about a shooting in the subway this morning.

All is jerky flow, go, next turn, go, step, go, move to the right go, now left, go, slow down, go, now forward, go, quickly, go, keep moving, go. . .All this done inside a screeching wailing concrete echo chamber of trains starting, stopping, doors opening, closing, loud speakers loud and unintelligible. Many secured within their own iPods being somewhere else as they direct their bodies through the maze.

I climb the last stairs to the platform for my train. Crowded in on all sides, there is a slight resentful body murmur at the person coming down what had just become the up staircase, an imperceptible movement by each person at the last moment that allows them to come down as others move up. Anything to keep the flow going.

Each of us in this alone, getting through the others to get to where we're going. Up on the platform, there is no space, the train being late. The platform has backed up and we all come to a stop. No flow. Now the static wait. We are frozen here, at the mercy of the MTA and their allotment of trains.

I begin to think of some of the trains I've waited for in my life – a sleeper train when I was a child that would take all night to get to a place called Maine where I would be in sleepover camp for a few weeks, the train into the city when I was in high school delivering furs into the fur market and getting others for my father, a suburban retail furrier, the train that was delayed to Bodh Gaya because the monsoon had washed out some of the track in India, and now an A train on the way to see my daughter uptown.

Slowly each person moves towards the edge to position themselves for when the train does come. There's a very careful assessing of space around oneself as in a traffic jam; to be close enough not to let anyone else in, but far enough away to give oneself wiggle room. We all finally come to a rest.

I glance around and scan the sea of us all. Just folks trying to get to work. Nothing special. No photo ops for politicians, no fashion shoots for models or movies. My eyes meet another scanner, a black woman in her 40s. Arranged, carefully groomed and costumed, her eyes show disinterest, habitual disdain and an implicit threat, "You do not want to mess with me." It must be learned and taught and practiced a thousand times over every day here in the city.

Her eyes move on with a slow closing and opening of the lids which dismisses me and goes on to the next unimportant person not worth focus. It is so institutionalized that I don't take it personally since it isn't personal. It's all part of the tedious passing show to be tolerated until something of interest happens.

How many Buddhas have come and gone unnoticed through my life while I've been busy on some quest or another? ("I came to you and you knew me not.")

Tap, tap, tap, the sound of a cane on the steps is heard through the din. A slight young unseeing woman is making her careful way up to the platform. The bustle continues all around her and she finally arrives.

A moment later the train arrives and the surge begins, everyone intent on getting on the train as soon as possible. As this happens, she of the disdainful gaze and I stay still. The blind woman is between us and we create a protective barrier around her. I gently touch her elbow and say, "I'll help you." The lady of the gaze moves in on the other side and we usher the woman on, gently moving others aside as we do.

An irritated young man looks at me sharply for I have dared to intrude on his defined space. He turns, glares and is ready to do battle in case he has been dissed. He sees it all in a glance, a light smile, nod and he moves to give her more space.

She moves her cane to find the subway car pole and reaches for it. A breath releases. She has made it this far. I give a small squeeze to her elbow. She nods slightly in my direction.

I spend the ride wondering about us all and how we become so formed in our different lives. So caught in our inner monologues. Then along comes the tapping of a cane to ask us what are we doing, who are we busy being.

Glancing around the car, my eyes again meet those of the first woman. She stops for a moment, nods to me with kindly eyes and about a tenth of a smile, then goes back behind her curtain and she becomes again a tough black woman not to be messed with.

A few stops later they both get off and I go back to wondering, who are we, what's going on here?

Chogyam Trungpa

It came to pass that Ananda and I decided to take Buddhist Refuge vows with Chogyam Trungpa Rinpoche. We went to where he was staying at the time which was Manhattan, Lower West Side. We ascended to his quarters where he was getting a haircut. He stopped when we entered and the three of us: He, Ananda, and I sat very close to each other. At one point he asked me, "Why do you want to do this?" I said I didn't know but he scared the shit out of me. I told him, "Nixon could kill my body but you could kill my mind." At which point he laughed delightedly and stroked my face. Ananda's response to Rinpoche's questions was less boisterous.

Later that evening, during the actual ceremony, we were to get up from the bleachers when our name was called. We were to walk across in front of him to the scribe who had our names written down on parchment both in English and Tibetan. We were to have the Tibetan Refuge name spoken out loud and translated for the first time. When mine was translated, I was opposite him. It was "Jigme Reltri" – the sword of fearlessness. We turned to each other laughing and pranammed (a formal salutation of respect).

Massage Comrades

His fingers were working their way around my back, searching out the knots of stored tension. Moving quickly, they would press and prod, then move on until a particularly tight one would be felt and he would dig in, working it, working it and then move on to another. It was a familiar feeling, these fingers working deeply and sometimes painfully into me. They signaled an ability to simply move right in. We had already come to an agreement; I was there to have him do his work, as he saw fit, and he would do it in his own manner, his own rhythm. He was Mark Jordan my favorite chiropractor.

We had gone past the formal niceties and had a good working relationship. He probed and prodded, and I surrendered into it as best I could although it often hurt much more than I would normally allow. I opened my body to him, and said, "I trust your intention and skill, do as you wish." He appreciated my trust and worked on me, reading, feeling, rooting his way along the pathways of my skin, muscles, connective tissue and bones. I would glance at his face and his eyes were usually closed, like a sightless massage person reading a face or a book. He or I would occasionally sigh or murmur or grunt at a particularly sore, contracted place.

This time, it was along the right side of my spine, in the middle of my back. As he pushed his thumb strongly along the contracted muscle, I felt myself removed to a time 20 years earlier when my then wife, Pat, and I were walking together in Manhattan. We were in the East 60's and had gotten tired of walking.

There was a small church ahead, and we went in to rest and get out of the sun. Great vaulted spaces, churches were usually good places to sit and be quiet. An oasis in the noisy activity of the city. The mind could soften and not feel constricted or on guard. We looked around and in our own separate way, found seats and sat a few rows apart.

It was cool and the pews were hard. No adaptation to modern comfort here. No cushions to soften the experience. This place was designed for the faithful to come and ruminate on their sins and make atonement in whatever fashion appropriate.

After a while, I glanced back and Pat was already somewhere in a quiet place inside herself. I sat in appreciation of her ability to sit, close her eyes and quickly have her darting busy mind get quiet and receive whatever was being given. I turned back and started to slow and deepen my own breath, a prelude to getting my own noisy mind a little more focused and quiet. A few breaths later, I started to sink down deeper inside and feel the rush of images and sensations become less demanding, less important, less compelling. Quieter, slower, opening. Watching my breath, it became softer and I was no longer so involved with where I was. I settled with ease into the sensation of my breathing.

Breathing, breathing, lightly and softly, the light around me darkening somewhat. I found that I was lying on a stone slab on my stomach with a deep, throbbing pain in the middle of my back. Looking slowly around, I saw dirt and straw around the slab and there was the thick smell of death and other wounded men around me.

I glanced over and saw my closest friend lying next to me also obviously wounded. We were casualties in a battle and had been brought here out of the way. There was blood all over us and I saw that my friend's scalp was partially laid bare. An axe had crushed part of his head.

My arm hung down and I lifted it slowly trying to reach toward my friend. As I looked at him, it became clear that we were dying. He had been wounded too deeply and I could feel my own crushed ribs and feel the blood running down my arm. The wound was too deep into my core to be healed and I had no longer the energy, the life to come back. I didn't know how long we had been there, but the battle and all that it had meant to us had retreated to a place so remote, it no longer concerned me.

I was getting quieter and quieter and my breath getting slower and more shallow. I was dying, more like water slowly dripping out of a bowl, soon to empty and come to an end, and then I would be dead. I reached over towards my comrade and tried to touch his face to tell him how much he had meant to me and that I loved him.

He reached over towards me with his eyes, not being able to move at all. He was already starting to go and I saw an imperceptible nod and smile of assent. My hand never reached him.

We had saved each other, nursed each other, fought for and with each other for a long time as soldiers. . .this war between nobles, fought by peasants. We had spoken few words, but we were thankful we had been thrown together in some filthy battle earlier and that we had been loving brothers since.

The only thing of importance now was to make sure he knew how much I honored and loved him, how grateful I had been and that I did not to have to go through it all and die alone. Him being there was somehow a perfect ending. My eyes began to cloud more as I saw him slowly dissolved into a darkness I was slowly floating into.

This was the Middle Ages in Europe and there was a religious war. We were peasants caught up in it with no choice about whether we fought or not. If we fought, we could go on living. To refuse was to be killed by a superior. Rebellion didn't exist. There was only submission and fighting to keep on living. No choices. It was all alright. We had lived and, as we knew would happen, we had been wounded and were now dying.

Slowly, I sank down into the dark quiet, deeper and deeper, very quiet, it lasted a long time. I lay back in peaceful gratitude.

After some time, I came out of my meditation and back into the church. Pat and I signaled to each other that we were done. We met at the church door, and clasped hands.

Pat was excited to tell me her meditation, which was exactly the same one I had! She was the dying soldier I tried to help in my meditation.

We were amazed that we were both in the same meditation, with the same specific details from so long ago. We continued down the New York City street, with a grin on our faces and a slight skip in our steps.

We were so glad to be with each other.

146

All of a sudden I was back on the chiropractor's table, astounded by the amount of baggage we all carry around hidden in our bodies.

Main Street Story

One fall day in 1999, I was walking down Main Street in New Paltz across from Gomen Kudosai, Yoko's restaurant. I had left Shop Rite and was walking to where I was living – a couple of rooms above the Laundromat on Plattekill. I glanced up and saw someone looking at me from a car leaving town. On the person's face was condemnation, wonderment and pity. Pity that I had lost a middle class life and how low I had fallen since I was walking and had no car.

I had not dropped out, but I was out of the middle class mainstream. I found myself in seemingly dire straits.

As I was walking, I recognized in that moment that I had done something similar years ago to another person. I smiled at the built in American classism and racism that was reflected in this interchange. I had been a carrier of that prejudice too.

Jeffrey, Bernie and Michael

When I was in college at Antioch in Ohio, I had a work-study job in a psychiatric hospital at Physicians and Surgeons, run by Columbia University in New York. I was an aide, and my uniform was white shirt, black pants, and a black bow tie. Three young men, exactly my age, who were patients there – Jeffrey, Bernie and Michael – took me under their wing. They even once threatened to take away my bow tie and name tag and make me one of them.

Fifteen years later, I found myself living at the Lama Foundation in Taos, New Mexico, with my wife, Ananda, and one-year-old daughter. At that point, the Lama Foundation was on the cutting edge of the culture for a certain group of people. The Lama Foundation, which still exists today, was an intentional community of seekers who lived together in a somewhat monastic life. It was great.

At the Foundation, we held Open Houses on Sunday when we provided a meal and tours of the place for visitors. As I was spooning out food one day, I recognized the men in front of me; they were Jeffrey, Bernie and Michael, and the four of us laughed – they used to be the inmates in the zoo and now they were here on the outside coming to visit me at the Lama Foundation.

What is going on here, I asked. Who is who? What is what? We all need a scorecard to keep track of what is happening.

Recently, one of my daughters and I saw a photograph of the Lama Foundation in the late 60s; the photograph showed our bell ringing center which we used for communication. She marveled that we had taken nose cones from the thermonuclear devices at the scrap heap across the valley at Los Alamos Laboratory.

Many years later, I applied for a job at Los Alamos to run their mental health program. Luckily, I did not take it since I could not separate what they were doing from mental health.

Grandpa Joe in Taos

In New Mexico, back in the early 70s, there was a very wise elder living in the Taos pueblo named Grandpa Joe Gomez. He was unusual because he was part of the peyote church that had obtained permission from the US government to use peyote in their religious rituals. Another aspect of his unusualness was his invitation to bring some westerners into his tepee. He was challenged but he said to others, "Some of them are ready to see new light and we have to foster that." The meetings were all night long where people would take peyote.

He was a tiny man, maybe 4' 10" and 80 pounds. In the tepee, where we would take peyote, made into cigarettes, he would make them out of corn husk and tobacco. It was believed that the smoke carried our prayers up to Chief Peyote.

One night, a man was going on and on tediously when Grandpa Joe snapped the fan he carried like a thunder clap. He pointed at the guy and said "It is ok mister; we are just people here – nothing fancy." The sigh of relief for the man and the rest of us was palpable.

I thank God for having met Grandpa Joe.

Christ at the Lama Foundation

The Lama Foundation always functioned as a base camp for people who were going further. I feel honored that I was there from 1971 to 1973.

After having lived at Lama for six months or so, I had become more comfortable. One Sunday, a man came to the open house with two young men beside him. He seemed to single me out for his attention and spoke to me in parables more than declarative sentences. I becoming less literal or rational became convinced within myself that he was in fact the Christ gathering people again.

His body was that of a working man and he was rough hewn – no tall white blonde Anglo Saxon Christ for me. Somehow or other, he was perfect. They were staying in a Winnebago just off the land and remained around for a while. Just before they came, Hari Dass, one of Maharaji's close devotees, had taught us that at any given time one nostril was more open than the other and to use the open nostril and turn it toward danger to protect oneself. The clear implication was that I was to go with Christ and his two sidekicks away on the bus. I was quite mesmerized.

Michael with Ananda and baby Amara
at Lama Foundation in Taos, 1971-73

At one point, I went down to the Winnebago and faced the choice point about whether I would go with him or not. When I put my hand on the railing to pull myself up into the bus, I remembered Hari Dass' teaching and turned my open nostril toward him. I told him that he should go away and I was not going with him. (Another indication of guardian angel intervention.)

I walked back up to Lama and went into the prayer room, a small dark room made of adobe, and curled up. I was whimpering when

Barbara Durkee happened in and sat close to me until I stopped whimpering. She held me on her lap and stroked my hair until I finally calmed down. She explained that there were people like me who were in full flower and whose energy emanated and that there were people like the man I thought was Christ who fed off the energy of others.

The two guys who were with him were somehow sallow and weak. It was as though he was a vampire and he had already eaten them. I did not realize until now how often and how well the guardian angels have taken care of me all my life.

Sasaki Roshi

When Ananda, Amara, and I first came to Lama in 1971, they were preparing to sit a sesshin – a seven day silent meditation – with Sasaki Roshi. As a trial by fire, the community decided to appoint me shoji, the interface between Roshi and the community.

When he first gathered us together on the first morning, Roshi said to all of us, "You must affirm your historical beings." This statement was given to a group of heavy hitters who were trying to get out of their bodies. What he said back then, made no sense to me, until now.

As part of being a shoji, it was expected that I would gather up or herd some of our more reluctant members and make sure that they were there for practice. One day, Frank Zero who was deeply immersed in esoteric spiritual teaching and therefore not my favorite person, was not at his usual sitting place so I went for him to the tepee set up near the edge of the property. He was a very different person from who I thought I was.

I entered his tepee, and told him he was missing Zazen. He said, "Fuck Zazen, I am sleeping. " I told him my job was to get him there. I jumped on him and wrestled with him. At one point, we

151

just started laughing and continued to wrestle. And then he said, "OK, that's enough; you win. Let's go be Buddhists."

About half way through the sesshin, it started snowing and we had to harvest the crops that day or lose them. It was given to me to ask Roshi's permission to suspend the sesshin. As I approached his garden hut where he was staying with his assistant, a tough German woman, I wondered where I was – Northern New Mexico, a snowstorm, an intentional community, and a sesshin with Roshi?

I knocked on the door, probably a little too loudly. When Roshi opened it, I blurted out the community's need. He said nothing, pulled me inside and made me take my boots and jacket off and wrapped me in a blanket and sat me down in what was his chair by the wood burning stove. Once seated, I attempted to explain the community's quandary of needing to gather the vegetables because of the snow while in the middle of a sesshin over which he, Roshi, had absolute power.

He looked at me with such loving kindness, put his fingers to his lips and said, "I know. Drink tea."

We finished our tea, somewhat leisurely, at which point he helped me put my coat and boots back on and assented. "Of course, we will start again tomorrow." I almost discerned a wink, but that would have been too much. Instead, we gave each other half bows, and I left.

Although being the shoji, I was not absented from many other sitting requirements and koan study with Roshi. He held the koan study in the library, and he filled the space although he was a small man. When it was my turn, I pranamed to him, and knelt down in Japanese fashion. He then asked me, "How do you manifest God while working as a carpenter." I had used up my bag of smart, clever intellectual bull shit already . He kept saying more Zazen, more sitting practice. I held a piece of wood and cut it in half in the air.

At this point, he threw me another one about flying a flag and I just dropped the wood and moved my hands like a flying flag.

He gave me two more , and I answered them immediately. "Ah Michael, you have woken up." But the last one I could not answer and stumbled down steps, the way you do two at a time. He smiled, and we pranamed to each other. He said "More Zazen."

O Roshi, O Roshi. Travel well and thank you.

*Michael and Ananda with baby Amara in woods
at Lama Foundation, Taos, New Mexico*

Maharaji Presence

Maharaji left his body or died in 1973. The full moon in September is used annually as his Bandhara, which is a feast gathering to celebrate his life. Devotees in India and America are honored to give a feast in his name. Local yogis in India are honored by being fed in his name and this all goes toward honoring his life. I found myself at one of these gatherings in New Mexico. We were lying on blankets on the grass watching a slide show of Maharaji. My experience was that it was repetition and very familiar. I was surrounded by Maharaji devotees and there was a general agreement that he was present. More than by image, his essence was blessing us. It was the first time that I felt myself fully a member of his family.

Henech Ha' Cohen

After sailing a boat from Key West, we had been in Tel-Aviv a couple of days when I went up the hill to Jerusalem and to the Western Wall. Somehow, I had become a member of one of 30 or so minyan who pray Shakrit at the Wall every morning. I was taken under the wing of a stranger named Ephraim who was the leader of one of these many minyans. He was a serious man.

After two weeks Ephraim said to me, "You are a good workman. You come early every day and you go to work but you don't bring your own tools." I had been borrowing tefillin from the Lubabitchers and Army guards who lent out tefillin at the Wall. Tefillin is a small leather box with Hebrew prayers inside. "You have to go up to Mayer Sharim (an Ultra-Orthodox community part of Jerusalem) and go to Henech Ha-Cohen and get kosher tefillin for 135 dollars" (which means hand-done, not printed, by an authorized sefer scribe). What he was asking me to get was $500 tefillin for $135. The other men in the minyan murmur how impossible that is.

Ephraim said it; so I did it. As I was walking up to Mayer Sharim, I put the kippah (a yarmulka) that I had been wearing in my pocket because I would rather have been taken for a dumb local tourist than one of them who is doing something clearly wrong. It was safer to be an outsider than some insider who should have known better. When I got to Mayer Sharim, I asked only men for directions out of safety and found myself outside an 1850s store 100 years later. There was rubble all around the buildings, the slippage in time was palpable. I stood at the open doorway, and surveyed where I had come to.

When I entered the store, there were all kinds of religious articles covering every single shelf and closet and of course, five or ten men who were there as a Greek chorus because going down to Henechs to hang out was always interesting.

I slowly went to the counter and waited respectfully. I was roughly 55, wearing a standard Israeli uniform of sandals, blue jeans, and a T-shirt; clearly with working man's hands. So I stood out as a funny one.

Henech came to the counter. He was all of 4'10", maybe 85 pounds. A wisp of a man. He slowly looked me over from head to toe, and paused until he decided something inside himself. "Nu?" He said. "Nu" was an invitation to state my case. I told him that Ephraim from the Western Wall had sent me for kosher tefillin for $135. This caused great rumbling among the Greek chorus of other Orthodox men. They said in Yiddish, which I do not speak, "What is this man doing? He is clearly a tourist, but not a tourist. He is asking for kosher tefillin for less than half price. What is he? Who is he? He seems to be buying tefillin for his kids but it is clear that it is for himself."

Henech looked at me again more carefully, more slowly and decided. "Nu," in a different inflection which meant that I was found worthy.

At this point, his son, a big soft bear of a man, a nice man, comes in (from stage right) to say in Yiddish again to the father, "It's crazy, he's a tourist! It is at least a $500 item that he wants. You can't give it to him." The father says to his son, "Outside, it says Henech Ha-Cohen. For now I set the prices. I'll die soon. Then it will have your name on it. Then you will set the prices. This man's okay. And Ephraim is a good man too."

Having decided despite the murmurings of the Greek chorus, he asks me where my father is from to see if I'm Ashkenaz or Sephardic. I tell him Ashkenaz and he begins to measure the straps. As he is measuring me and measuring the straps, he asks me, "Tallis?" To which I said, "No." (A tallis is a fringed prayer shawl.) The straps tie the tefillin to my forearm and forehead. He put the tallis into the bag anyway. Another $50. At the end, he puts them all in the bag, kisses me on the forehead and sends me away. As I walked back to Jerusalem and the Wall, I realized that I just had my Bar-Mitzvah. Wonderful to be embraced by a loving grandfather.

The Jerusalem Wall

I helped deliver a boat for an Israeli national back to Israel from Key West, Florida, with a few other guys. They, Christians, did the obligatory tourist tour: took a taxi up to Jerusalem, got their attendance tickets and their minds stamped, and went home. The owner had bought us all tickets to fly back to the States the day we got to Israel. I turned mine in and got a postponement knowing that God had not gone through all that trouble to get me to Israel to leave so soon. I helped the owner deliver the boat up the coast to a new marina a few miles away and did a few other things on the boat to prepare it.

We were done with each other, he paid me and essentially evicted me. All okay. There was nothing else for me to do but go up to Jerusalem, to the Wall (the nominal center of Judaism). It turns out I got to Jerusalem and the Wall at mid-day. No one seemed to be around because it was the heat of the day. I went to the Wall. I was embarrassed by how much I strove for true "spiritual experience."

I began to cry and I knew that it wasn't the history of the Jewish people, or the Holocaust, or the usual suspects inside of me. I recognized those. This was different and I didn't recognize it. I thought, thought, felt. What was this?

Finally, I recognized that I was weeping for both the shame and innocence of the crimes I had committed against myself to get by as a skinny-Jewish-kid, post-holocaust in Christian America. Never denying my Judaism but also learning how to carefully negotiate the anti-Semitism in my life. Quiet, subdued, but potentially lethal. I vowed "Never Again."

The Affirmation

Pat Rodegast, my second wife, the channel for a spirit named Emmanuel, and I would meditate every morning. She was not particularly in to Maharaji but that was okay with me. One morning she said, "I don't know how to tell you but it seems that Maharaji is here." I had separately been experiencing his presence but assumed that it was me conjuring the experience rather than him really being there.

I had gone through a very painful 20 years of believing that I had not gone to meet with him earlier in India when I had been chosen and called because I held back at the time due to my lack of faith. I condemned myself for cowardice until I heard a story about him threatening to turn some of his deepest devotees against him unless they did their work duties. Recognizing that he could easily have paved the way for me to be with him, I had realized that the cause of my not going to meet him had been him rather than me. . .a complete revolution in my thinking.

When it was established that I could speak to him, I asked him if he was the same man who I had seen at age seven, to which he replied, "Yes. I have been with you all of your life." Then I asked him, "Why wouldn't you let me be with you?" Implying, face to face in India, 20 years ago. He answered, "You would have become too attached to his form." Meaning, I would have fallen too deeply in love with a form of Maharaji and lost all sense of boundaries, which was true. He, of course, was right. I would have become a perfect devotee, telling myself and everyone how to do it the "right" way.

I was weeping from the affirmation that the central legend of my life seemed to be actually true. That the yearning of my life had some purpose to it. It was not dismissable.

It was during this darshan when I asked him for a mantra. After a long pause, Maharaji said emphatically, "I don't know. . .I love." I have since taken on that mantra to be mine. . .and the title of this book. I see this as Maharaji's central teaching to me. . .I take it on gladly.

VII. Other Experiences

Author's Note: *This is a talk I gave to the Kol Hai, a Jewish renewal congregation in New Paltz, NY, at its Feb. 1, 2019 Shabbat service at Woodland Pond, transcribed by Zachary Rausch*

Covenant of Connectedness

I have been very fortunate as my body has come apart because they, the beings who run my life, God and all God's consorts, have given me glimpses into what I experience as being truth. This is very different from my normal operating mind. Although still pretty clear, my operating mind is no match for what I am seeing. I am so thankful for it. Part of what I want to do is recognize what is happening to me and share it with you because you don't hear much from people this close to death. I tell people that it will happen Tuesday at two o'clock, but I am not sure which Tuesday.

My understanding is that the word "Israel" means "One who wrestles with God." And that is not a strength or endurance test; it is a walking with God. Everyone here is a wrestler with God and I honor you for that.

All that is going through my mind tonight is the humility I feel being with you. Thank you for creating this space. No matter what we think we are doing, we are coming forth to renew our covenant. Not as the Jewish people particularly. Well, maybe. We are renewing the covenant of connectedness. We renew God.

But what I want to say with full disclosure is that I might be guilty of apostasy tonight. I apologize for it if it offends anyone. Every time that we love and we move toward that open-hearted compassionate loving, we renew God. God becomes more real and becomes vaster. Thank you all for doing that because it is clear that you acknowledge our correctedness, thereby expanding God, no matter what it seems like to you.

Do you know what a hechsher is? It is a seal. It is when a Rabbi gives authority to a person to sell whatever is kosher. We spend our lives, our whole lives, striving for hechsher. We get a degree, get a high school diploma, get a college degree, get a blessing from a high being. Oh I'm friends with so and so - that's a hechsher. Because now I am worth listening to. Otherwise I would not be worth listening to. What happens is that everyone in this room has perceptions that are so clear and so fine that they get to the heart of the matter of things. But we haven't got the hechsher we think we should have, so we do not honor our own authority.

This may piss some of you off. Here we go. Nothing is wrong. I am dying. I mean, within a few months. I am dwindling down but nothing is wrong. It's being worked out perfectly and I celebrate what is happening. I am being shown what comes next because I finally shut up enough so I can feel, I can hear, I can sense things. I am soft enough to receive these insights.

I was employed by an extremely wealthy man who was head of a bank with over 1,000 employees. It was a big deal. I asked him, "What do you do all day? The image in the comic books is that you have your feet on the desk and count your money. I know you don't do that. What do you really do?" He laughed for a second and then got very serious and said, "I deal with trivial matters of great importance." We all spend our lives dealing with trivial matters that we make very important, but every now and then we get a vision, we get a notion, we get a sense of how it can be; how it really is beyond our imagination. How it could be. And we touch that every Shabbat, for which I am very grateful. Nothing is wrong.

I have a puzzle in my head of weird little pieces that are mine. Each one of us has a puzzle that we made up. Out of a few extraordinary experiences that each of us have had, out of the millions and trillions of mind moments that we have, we build the universe out of these minutiae, these tiny, tiny details. We develop a whole worldview from these moments and we devote our lives to them. Look at them, lovingly and gently.

I may be mistaken but my understanding is that we have a word for sin, which is a big deal in Christian America. The Jewish word for *sin* is one that means off the mark; missing the mark. That is a fascinating concept because we all know when something misses the mark. We all can feel it. We each have a perfection within us. We might not be able to articulate it but we are able to feel it. Bless us all so that we stay on the mark. So when we do and we are with another person, it is truly, hail fellow well met; namaste; there is loving truth that exists in that moment.

There is a saying that when two or more are gathered in my name, I shall be there. It is ascribed to Jesus of Nazareth. I have no idea about the provenance of that phrase. But the notion of two or more gathering in the name of love. God is there. God is nigh.

I have a grandson. A beautiful kid; a lovely kid. He and I were going to start *mensch* training together. I figured I might have one or two things to say to him. I thought and I thought and I thought. What do I have to say? What did I learn?

The first principle of mensch training is own what you do. If you won't own it, don't do it. Own what you do. Stand behind it. Bring to it a sense of perfection.

I want to tell you something about owning your own authority. I was telling Shir about this insight. About really owning ourselves because I see people giving up their authority all day everywhere. Because you have to, you have to, you have to. That is the regret that old people feel as they look back and see that they gave it away for nothing. A precious life force that all of us have. Honor it.

Shir = Rabbi of Kol Hai congregation of New Paltz

Mensch = A Yiddish saying meaning a person of integrity

Hechsher = A hechsher means "prior approval." a rabbinical product certification, qualifying items (usually food)

At War With the World

It's funny. We have been talking about right and wrong, good and bad, correct and incorrect. It stimulates in me a recognition that I have spent most of my life up until just recently being at war with the world.

If it wasn't going right, I had to control and manipulate it in order to make sure that things came out right. And now, I guess I have much more faith, whatever that means, than I used too.

I believe that things are designed to come out right on a much, much grander scale. Human life has maybe a 100 years. That is nothing. Absolutely nothing in relation to eternity. Things are designed in a more positive way than I used to think.

Burial

The question about my burial is whether to be buried in the Jewish section or in the regular section of the cemetery.

The Jewish section of the cemetery is by the road and is the least attractive part of it. It feels like a ghetto to me. And I know that I have been involved with stuff outside of Judaism such as Hinduism, Buddhism, and my own spiritual experiences.

It is part of my Bodhisattva activity to engage *other:* to engage outsiders. I have not lived a narrow, specific, Jewish life. For these reasons, I am seriously thinking about being buried out in the regular cemetery (which has got its own stuff to it). But even if I am buried in the regular cemetery, I would like to have a Jewish ceremony. That is clear to me. That is my home out of which I had come. I want to go back to that in the end.

For the last 20 years, I haven't thought about disposing of a body. Whenever asked, I would automatically say "cremated" without having really thought about it. When a friend mentioned that it took about 60 gallons of fuel for modern cremation, it seemed ecologically appalling to me, and that the old way was more attractive. Simply put the body into the ground and let things happen. So I am deciding to bury my body in the ground in the end.

Lastly...

While reading this, you may be somewhat overwhelmed by all my experiences. They were not continuous. I spent a lot of confused downtime feeling that I, like you, was simply lost. My life has been a series of experiences filled with grace. So is yours. Use my life and this book to help you, not to hurt yourself. Please don't compare. Rather, learn to sing your own song.

About Michael Projansky

When Michael Projansky was seven years old in 1946, he had a very strong feeling that he was born to love all human beings. He also had a clear vision of a wise man up in the clouds, whom he did not discover until 20 years later was Maharaji -- his spiritual guide for the rest of his life.

After graduating from Antioch College in 1962 and earning his PhD in Clinical Psychology at Adelphi University in 1966, he taught psychology at Southampton College on Long Island for two years, getting married in 1968 and raising three daughters. He lived at the Lama Foundation, an intentional spiritual community near Taos, New Mexico, from 1971 to 1973 with his wife Ananda, and then became teaching assistant to Ram Dass in the first summer of Chogyam Trungpa Rimpoche's Naropa Institute at Boulder, Colorado, in 1974.

Projansky made one trip to India in 1976, having remarkable experiences, some of which are described in this book. After practicing psychological therapy in the New Paltz, New York, area, he worked for ten years in the Caribbean as a bare boat skipper and boat delivery captain. He spent his next 20 years sailing a 38-foot yacht for a wealthy New York businessman from Nova Scotia to the Caribbean from 1997 to 2017, when his rare ALS disease stopped his sailing and he moved into the Woodland Pond nursing facility in New Paltz. There he charmed all the nurses and a steady stream of visiting friends, and explored for himself the space between life and death in a calm state of curiosity about his next voyage.

About this book

"I Don't Know...I Love" was the mantra given to Michael by his spiritual guide Neem Karoli Baba (Maharaji). It is an analogy of his life long struggle to raise his consciousness and daily work from rational knowledge of the world and his professional practice of psychological therapy to loving kindness for everyone he meets, with his daily work meditation and spiritual practice.

This book is a journal of Michael Projansky's life voyages on land and sea. Chapters on visiting dying people with a dedicated Hospice doctor, and surviving a 2,750 mile sailing trip across the Atlantic with three drunken Englishmen, were written years ago by the author himself. The rest of this book contains remarkable stories told by Projansky to his many friends, two of whom wrote them down in June and July of 2019, so that this book could be published quickly before he died. He wanted to see it and give it to family and friends at his memorial service.